MARIAH
of the Spirits
AND OTHER SOUTHERN GHOST STORIES

Sherry Austin

The Overmountain Press
JOHNSON CITY, TENNESSEE

Book design by Cherisse McGinty
Jacket design by Bill May, Jr.
Edited by Jason Weems

Hardcover ISBN 1-57072-239-0
Trade Paper ISBN 1-57072-231-5
Copyright © 2002 by Sherry Austin
Printed in the United States of America
All Rights Reserved

1 2 3 4 5 6 7 8 9 0

For Willie Reavis Owens: mother, friend, salt of the earth.

AUTHOR'S NOTE

Special thanks to: the North Carolina Arts Council and the National Endowment for the Arts; Janie Plumley and Clint Plumley for their efforts in preserving the folklore and music of the Dark Corner in northern Greenville County, South Carolina; Elizabeth Wright, my publisher, for opening the door to me; Jason Weems, for conscientious editing; Carolyn Sakowski, for tireless advice and encouragement in the very early stages of this project; and to Rick Austin, my beloved, for everything.

CONTENTS

INTRODUCTION

A ghost story, if it is nothing else, ought to be fun. It ought to make us feel the way we do when we see trees bent by the wind before a storm, hear the scuttle of dry leaves across a cobblestone walk, or drive a long, desolate stretch of swamp road where we've heard a mysterious hitchhiker walks on rainy nights. But a ghost story can be more than that. Good supernatural literature, said folklorist Dorothy Scarborough, gives us "entrance to immortal countries."

Writers of ghost stories are continually asked if they believe in ghosts. As for literal belief, I am both skeptic and believer. I am wary of charlatans, and take TV psychics and shows about America's most haunted places with a grain of salt. I believe that debunkers of psychic phenomena, like the Amazing Randi and the late astronomer Carl Sagan, make the very valid point that the world we know, or think we know, invokes more than enough wonder to blow our minds, so why all the interest in spoon-bending, UFOs, and spirits? I agree, and yet I have found that the more I observe the wonders of the world we do know—the world that unfolds right before our eyes, the universe revealed to us by science—the more I believe in the proverbial unseen, the unknown, the penumbral zone that lies just outside our senses, the world revealed to us in our dreams and stories. I feel it is foolishness to believe everything we hear, but it is the height of arrogance to think we know everything, too.

In an expanding universe of black holes and superstrings, all things seem possible. After all, it was Einstein himself who said that "Our notions of physical reality can never be final." Scientist, rocket engineer, and visionary Dr. Werhner von

Braun once said: "Science has found that nothing can disappear without a trace. Nature does not know extinction. All it knows is transformation. . . . Everything science has taught me—and continues to teach me—strengthens my belief in the continuity of our spiritual existence after death. Nothing disappears without a trace."

The idea of spirit existing independently of the body has never been exorcised from our collective consciousness. The concept of spirit and the belief in ghosts saturates our ancient and contemporary folklore, mythology, and religion. In Chinese tradition the seventh lunar month is known as "Ghost Month," when the gate opens between this world and the spirit world. The Celtic New Year was the time when the veil between the worlds of the living and the dead was thinnest, when communion between the two was possible; no matter that fewer people believe it now, the remnants of that notion survive in our Halloween observances. Scriptures of the great religions include accounts of spirits interacting with humanity. In chapter 28 of 1 Samuel, King Saul goes to the Witch of Endor to get her to call up the spirit of the dead prophet Samuel. In the fourth chapter of Job is his well-known account of a visiting spirit. In classical Islam, the *jinn* have many characteristics of ghosts: they are usually unseen by people, are free to do good and evil and interact with the living. Buddhism has its realm of hungry ghosts; Hindu mythology has its *vetala*, ghosts who haunt cemeteries and ruins. Taken altogether, that's a great cloud of witnesses to an ancient and enduring belief.

The stories in this collection arise from the soil of the American South, a place writer Flannery O'Conner called "Christ-haunted." It is, even today, a place infused with spirit. Spiritual seekers swarm to what is thought by many to be a great mystical vortex in Western North Carolina. Yet mainstream Christianity remains stalwart, many Appalachian folk beliefs hang on, and remnants of the animistic beliefs of our African ancestors can still be found on the coasts of the Carolinas and Georgia.

Though the Old South of some of these stories is itself a

ghost—and is hard to even imagine among all the corporate parks, residential developments, and golf resorts—you still might get a glimpse of it around the bend of a country road. You can still see it in the chimney left standing after a long-abandoned homestead has crumbled to dust, in laundry strung on a line and flapping white against a black storm cloud, in a hillside graveyard where the dead are buried facing east so they may rise to meet the resurrected Christ on the prophesied last day.

In isolated places, graveyard workday is still observed, with the unspoken assumption that the dead stay in their place. In old seaport towns and in rural pockets between exclusive beach resorts, you can still find tiny graveyards where tobacco tins, eyeglasses, and medicine bottles have been placed on the graves to deter restless spirits. There too you can still sometimes see a bottle tree in a small sandy front yard, its limbs graced with colorful bottles catching the sun, gleaming like stained glass. The spirits trapped in the bottles still whistle and moan when the wind blows. And there are still a few less-traveled byways where your headlights might pick up that hitchhiker, in a distinctly Southern incarnation, walking that long, lonesome road. . . .

MARIAH
of the Spirits

Mariah walked the sandy coastal back road with quick long strides. Her coarse black braids hung wild down her neck; her homespun dress hung limp on her body. The air was so damp and thick she felt like she was swimming through it. She wished she could run like the wind, the way she could when she was a young girl. That's what her name meant, her Mama had told her a long time ago—Mariah: the wind. But she could only walk as fast as she could walk. She had a long way to go before sunrise.

Mariah was frailer than she once had been. Her back was worn as an old pack mule's, though she was not yet forty. Her feet were worn like the shoes she'd flung off two miles back. Time was she could work from "can see to can't see, and into the night if need be." She could carry big sweetgrass baskets on her head—baskets heavy with pecans she'd gathered up from the grove, blackberries she'd picked from bushes by the roadside, herring she'd caught with a net in the river. Mariah, when young, could carry a heavily laden basket on her head with such grace that Loomis, a field hand, would drop his hoe, would risk the whip, just to stop and watch the long, strong muscles in her back working like a panther's. Mariah had big dreamy eyes and dreamy ways, but she could work like a horse. On her back Mariah had carried sheaves of rice, bales of cotton, and babies.

But that night she could not be burdened. That night Mariah carried only three things: between her breasts—a fistful of cash money to bribe the hangman; in her left pocket—a flint rock and a little piece of steel to start a fire with; in the waistband of her skirt—a kitchen knife with which she had decapitated many a live chicken with one deft flick of her wrist, so quick and clean the beady eyes of the dead chickens had stared up at her dumbstruck. And she would not flinch before using it on her master's patroller if he caught up with her and threatened to hold her back. She had to get to Mosi before they hung him at first light.

Mosi. Nineteen years ago her firstborn son, Mosi, had been foretold to Mariah in a noonday dream. She had been out in the field picking cotton on a white-hot day. Mariah, with child by Loomis, felt sick and faint, and fell down in a swoon. She sank right down in the high cotton and fell spinning down into a deep dark place. The roll of thunder roused her out of sleep. She sat up, opened her eyes; the sun had darkened and the wind had picked up. White dust blew like snow off the cotton. Down the furrow, about as far away as she could throw a rock, stood a little boy, not quite a year old she guessed, his shirttail barely covering his naked bottom. What a picture he made standing there, his brown face with white tufts of cotton all around it. He had one arm stretched out, feeling of a cotton boll with his fingers while he watched her. She had never seen a boy so pretty. Something wild, teasing, ticklish about his eyes. She knew all the field hands' babies, but this one she did not know. She sat there hugging her knees, watching him, smiling. He winced when the sharp boll pinched his fingers. He jerked his hand away but didn't cry. He looked at it, saw it had drawn blood, and stuck his fingers in his mouth. "Come here, sugar," she said, waving him toward her, but he turned, toddled off, and disappeared in the high cotton. Mariah ran all through the fields looking for him, calling for him, even after the lightning and thunder had started, even when rain came down hard and heavy and all the other field hands went running for shelter under the shed roof. Loomis had run high-stepping through the fields and the rain after her, had picked her up and hauled her, legs kicking, to the shed. "Ain't been no child out in the field today," he said. "You crazy, baby."

Come January that next year she gave birth to a boy, to that same boy. She knew it was the same one from the minute he opened his eyes, even if Loomis and Old Shoog didn't believe it. Everybody from the quarters came to see Mariah sitting by the fire in her cabin, holding that baby. It was something to see. They'd never seen a girl such a fool over a baby. Even the missus came from the Big House, said she'd never laid eyes on such a pretty child. Mariah named him Mosi. The name meant firstborn. And when he was nigh on a year old, she could see, not that she had ever doubted, that he was that same boy she'd seen in the cotton field that day, every inch of him. He had been foretold to her in a dream.

Mariah made a bottle tree just for Mosi. She saved bottles of bear grease and bitters, washed them with lye soap, and hung them on the stripped limbs of a scrub pine. While Mariah was in the field, Old Shoog, the old, old slave woman who looked after the field workers' children, would sit Mosi in the sand and watch him watch the sunlight flash through the bottles and make rings of blue-green, dark green, amber, and yellow on the ground. Mosi's eyes would dance around following them. He would squeal, grab at them with his hands. The spirits trapped inside the bottles whistled and moaned in the wind, hummed like a chorus. That would pacify him better than singing a lullaby, Shoog said.

Early and late in the day, when the sun didn't bear down so hard, Mariah carried him to the field in a sack on her back. While she wore herself down picking cotton, she dreamed that he would not have to. "The little baby gone home," she'd sing, "the little baby gone along, for to climb up Jacob's ladder. . . ." She sneaked away some of the ABC blocks the master's children played with, even though if the missus caught Mosi playing with them she'd give Mariah a whipping. She didn't know how to read or how to teach Mosi to read, but she thought getting Mosi letters to look at was a start. Wouldn't be no ordinary field hand, not her firstborn. Wouldn't be no boy fanning flies off Master's children. Mariah had dreams, big dreams—one day he'd raise an insurrection, would lead big numbers of his people to freedom.

"You working all that up in your head," Old Shoog said when Mariah ventured to tell her about Mosi's destiny.

"He's going to be somebody big someday," Mariah said.

"You got other chillun," Shoog warned her after Mariah had birthed Silas, Henry, and Mary. Shoog's face was stern whenever she watched Mariah buzzing around Mosi like a fly around sorghum while her other children hung around like hounds hoping she'd throw them a bone. But Mosi was her firstborn, she told Shoog, and had been foretold to her in a dream.

Mariah walked on through the night. Where she walked now, limbs of live oak trees met in the middle of the road, and moss drooped from the trees like hags' hair. Mariah felt like there was nothing between the road and the bones of her feet. She stopped and fell to her knees, to rest her feet, to catch her breath. She turned and looked back over the road she had traveled and let out a sob like a dog's bark. The long sandy road soaked up the moonlight. As far back and as far ahead as she could see, the road stretched on and on like a straight white arrow shot through the dark. She had walked a long way since nightfall, but she still had a long way to go to reach the hanging place by sunrise.

The moon had climbed high and had whited out the stars by the time she reached the railroad tracks that marked the halfway place. Mariah was afraid of the halfway place. Near those same railroad tracks the woods of three plantations came within a mile of each other. Patrollers crawled in that place like ticks, and many runaways would take the snake's way through the swamps rather than step one foot where Mariah now walked.

Mariah crossed the railroad tracks and ran along the edge of the road for half a mile, hurrying to get that place behind her. She arrived at the place where two roads crossed. Everybody knew that haints and plat-eyes could hover thick as mosquitoes at crossroads, appearing—when they let themselves be seen at all—as floating lights, goats, horses, men on horseback. Where the roads crossed, Mariah could not hug the edge of the woods; she had to fly out into the middle, knowing her pale dress picked up the moonlight, knowing she could be spotted from any of four directions from half a mile or more away. Mariah knew she should fly over the road, looking straight ahead, to get through the crossroads as quick as she could. But halfway over she looked from side to side and saw a globe of golden light floating like a small sun in the woods at the edge of the westerly road.

The light barreled down the road with the thunder of horse hooves. Mariah slipped into the woods, her feet pounding the soft sandy earth, her heart pounding in her chest, her breath ragged. She followed a narrow footpath through the thick palmetto and twisty undergrowth, past a small, forgotten-looking graveyard. She wound around through the graves, causing gnats to swarm up out of the undergrowth, causing something as scared as she was to scurry away into the woods. She ducked behind a tree, laid head and hands flat to the ground, and stuck her rump up in the air like a sleeping baby. The horse hooves slowed to a clip-clop, clip-clop, and the rider guided the horse along the edge of the woods, then down the narrow path to the graveyard. Mariah swallowed her breath. From behind the tree she couldn't see the rider or his face, only the big pool of gold light that fell over the ground as he raised his lantern. The light stopped just shy of the tree Mariah crouched behind. The rider held the lantern up higher still, and a broader arc of light swung her way. Patroller or plat-eye? "Oh, sweet Jesus!" Mariah mumbled. She clutched the knife by the handle, stayed facedown, and didn't take a good breath until the last sound of horse hooves faded away.

Mariah knew the ways of patrollers, if patroller it was. She knew he would likely ride a little ways down a side path and wait for her awhile. So no matter how much she was in a hurry, she knew it paid her to tarry a little. She sat there, her back to the tree, her arms stretched over her knees. She caught her breath and pressed her hand to her thudding heart to get it to slow down. Just enough moonlight filtered through the pines that she could see a little of what was around her. It was a slave graveyard. She could tell because most of the stones didn't have names written on them, much less when the people buried there had been born or had died. No sweet promises of the Hereafter like you find on white folks' graves.

Seashells lined the outer edges of the shallow mounds. They were put there to fence in the spirits. Mariah noticed cracked flowerpots, broken dishes, broken bottles of tonic, shattered spectacles, bent tobacco tins, all things that the dead had used in life, all put there to quiet their spirits after death. All had been broken or dented, not so nobody would steal them, but to show that ties with the world have been broken, to show the spirits they must not come back again. Mariah picked up a cracked blue bottle that she thought would look pretty on her bottle tree back home. Blue bottles were hard to come by. But she dropped it right back where she found it. She knew she wouldn't be going back. She wouldn't have taken it anyway, because to rob a grave was to rile a spirit.

On the road once more, Mariah hugged the edge of the woods and watched the moon cloud over, then clear again. The same moon shone down on Mosi. Mariah had a picture in her mind of Mosi, hands bound, feet shackled, lying face-down on a dung-packed floor in Joyner's stable, where they would keep him until morning came and it was time for the hanging. One side of his head lay flat on the floor. The eye on the other side of his face stared, rarely blinking, at a window cut high in the barn. She knew Mosi looked up at the same moon as his mama did, and, for some reason she didn't understand, that gave Mariah some hope. Mariah prayed that Mosi's hands and feet would slip the shackles, that he'd cut and run, as Silas had heard he had done many times. Mosi could weasel out of a steel trap.

Mosi had been wise before his time. When he was old enough to talk, he'd tell Mariah about things that happened before he was born. One day he sat at the kitchen table over his bowl of hominy and told her how when she was a little girl she'd sat by the fire picking seeds out of the cotton. Now how could he know about that when Master got the gin before Mosi was ever born? Nobody had handpicked seeds out of cotton for years. Shoog said he must have heard them talking about it. She said it even though they all knew they were too beat down of an evening to sit around and chew the fat about what went on that day, much less days gone by. But then Mosi looked up at Shoog and reminded her how she used to gather up leaves from the oak trees to make a hat to wear to church. Now, that was something Shoog had not done since she was a young girl, fifty or sixty years before Mosi was born. Shoog closed her eyes, shook her head. "That boy going to make trouble for hisself one day," she said. "He got too much sense to keep in line." Shoog warned Mariah to watch him. She said a slave woman better watch her children, better see they don't rock the boat, stoke the wrath of the master, and get sold away.

But Mariah couldn't do that. He would get caught drawing in the sand, teaching himself to cipher, fishing on Sunday, running off without a pass. Get a whipping and do it all over again. Mosi was ten years old when they sold his daddy. Before they took Loomis away, he warned Mariah, "Better see that boy hoes a straight row."

"Might as well try to keep creek water in a sieve," Mariah told him, choking back tears.

Mosi ran away to the woods and hid there for weeks before a patroller hauled him home. The overseer whipped him, making scars over the ribbons of scars already there. It nearly killed Mariah to watch it and she was afraid for Mosi, but she was proud of him, too. Lord knew couldn't no milksop boy do what she believed her Mosi was destined to do. He was seventeen years old the day the overseer cussed him over the way he was picking, and Mosi had raised a hoe over his head and would have killed the overseer if the other hands hadn't tackled him just in time. After that Master wrote Mosi up as trouble and sold him for four hundred and fifty dollars to the next cattle drover who happened by.

Two years passed. In that time she never heard from or about Mosi, except for suspect scraps of news Silas brought home sometimes. But she prayed she'd see him again one day. For reasons Mariah was not given to know, the master's fortune had started to dwindle. There had been talk of it in the fields. Mariah's daughter, Mary, who'd had two babies before she was seventeen, was advertised and sold as "good breeding stock," and her boy Henry was sold off too. Silas was all she had left, a frail boy with sleepy eyes and a slow mind, not much use in the field or at the Big House, so the Master's son used him for a horse boy. Silas wasn't much use to Mariah, either, except for the tales he repeated, mainly what he had heard about Mosi. Mariah was starved for any scrap of news about her firstborn.

As a horse boy Silas spent a lot of idle time on the road, at other plantations, and at markets where other slaves talked and told stories. He heard a lot, saw a lot, and he'd bring it home to Mariah, knowing she couldn't hear enough about Mosi. Mariah was never sure if all of what Silas said was true. He knew any tale he told about Mosi would get his mama's attention like nothing else, and he'd told just enough truth in the past that she listened to what he said no matter how wild and unlikely it sounded. Mosi had escaped from that drover and was on the loose, he told her one day. Mosi had been captured again, was seen waist deep in mud digging a canal near Okefenokee Swamp. He'd been seen on the auction block in Savannah, seen hiding in the woods, caught working up an uprising. He'd slipped out of stocks, jails. Mosi had been lynched one week, seen again the next. Mosi, they said, could worm his way up from six feet under the ground. The tales Silas brought home! Mariah listened, wondered, and waited for Mosi's knock on the door.

Then one day Silas came home with the tale that Arvel Joyner had bought Mosi. She looked him hard in the face. "Silas, you ain't lying to me? Mosi's at the Joyners'? You've seen him there?" Silas said he had. Mariah could hardly contain her joy. The Joyner place was just half-a-day's drive by wagon, a day's walk. Might be Master would give her a pass to go there. Might be she'd slip away and go whether he gave her one or not.

But before she had a chance to ask for a pass or think about slipping away, Silas brought home bad news—they had accused Mosi of murdering Joyner's overseer. The overseer had beaten a pregnant field worker until the blood ran; that night the overseer was found on the road, bludgeoned to death. Any one of the field workers might have killed him; but it got laid on Mosi, and he wouldn't be one to deny it and let it get put on somebody else. He would be hanged at sunrise the next morning. Mariah had grabbed Silas, had shaken him until his eyes rattled. "Now, you know for the truth it's Mosi they were talking about? You know for the truth it's this morning? This coming morning?"

Time was Mariah wouldn't have stolen a scrap of stale cornpone from the master's kitchen. But for some time now, whenever she was called from the fields to help out at the Big House, she slipped into the dining room and pilfered from the stash of bills the missus kept in a sideboard drawer. Mariah had dreamed big dreams of buying back Mosi, if it took all the years she had left. "You crazy, baby," she knew Loomis would say. But that night, after Silas had spoken, she had taken the money from where she'd hidden it—an empty jar that had once held tonic—and had tucked it into her bodice. She slid the knife into the waistband of her skirt. She waited until the last lamp was extinguished up at the Big House, until all the windows to all the shacks in the quarters were blank as closed eyes. Then Mariah had followed the back roads all through the night, past fields wide as the world, into the edge of the cypress swamp. Finally, just before daylight, she approached the hangman's place.

The shack where the hangman lived was built up on pilings at the swamp's edge, just as she remembered it. Mariah had been to a hanging at that same place when she was a girl. In the winter, when there wasn't so much to do around the place, Master gave the slaves passes to go to hangings, especially when the condemned was a slave who had started trouble. Mariah remembered the twisted, gleeful face of the hangman. She remembered standing at the foot of the gallows, squeezing her eyes shut as the hangman slipped the noose around the condemned man's neck. She had jumped when the trapdoor was released, had felt sick hearing the sound of the rope as the body rocked back and forth, back and forth, after the man fell. She thought when she opened her eyes it would be all over, but it had taken the man twelve minutes to die. He fought for breath right before her eyes. His mouth and nose had turned purple, and his eyes had bulged.

Now, as Mariah approached, the moonlight glowed from the tin roof of the hangman's place. The water was up and the house sat right over the water. The house looked like if you gave it a push it would float clean away. A live oak limb stretched so far across the water it was a wonder the tree had not toppled over from the weight of it. Mariah remembered hearing that was the old hanging tree. Many were hung there before the hangman built the gallows that stood a few yards past the house. The rope was there now, waiting for Mosi.

The sun came up, turning the tin roof of the shack and the water around the cypress knees red as blood. Nobody was there yet. There was no mob gathering, no black-hatted preacher ready to mouth words from an open Bible. Joyner's men had not come yet, as they soon would, dragging Mosi in shackles to the gallows. There was time to bribe the hangman.

Mariah stood at the door and held up her fist. She didn't hesitate a minute before she knocked, even though she was a runaway, even though the hangman, when he saw her, would most likely be thrilled to death to turn her in for running away, for stealing money from the master. Mariah knew she would be stripped naked, put in the stocks, whipped until the blood ran, or worse. Mariah beat her fist on the door.

When somebody finally came out, it was not the hangman she remembered from her youth. This man's face was not twisted and mean like the one she remembered, but instead was long, with sideburns curling thick at the sides. He looked like a sheep. "Hep you?"

"I come a long way." Mariah's voice came out small, like the whimper of a puppy. All the hours of walking, worrying, grieving were telling on her now. She could hardly stand. She could hardly ask him, for fear of what he would say.

"You hanging a man this morning?"

The sheep-faced man watched her dumbly, like a sheep would. "What's it to you?"

Mariah reached her hand down between her breasts and took out the money.

He eyed the money like it might be a snake. "You meaning to try to bribe me? What is it you think I can do?"

"I don't know. I've heard tell a hangman can fiddle with the noose somehow, make it look like the man's dead when he's not, to please the law, to satisfy the crowd."

"You heard wrong. Ain't up to me to second-guess the law, or go against the mob. Besides, ain't no hangin' today," he said. "Not here. They was a hangin' yesterday. Drew a big crowd. Looks like you're a day late."

Mariah closed her eyes, covered her mouth with one hand, and hung on the door with the other. "Then I got to know where my boy's body is! And I come prepared to pay for it!" Mariah, eyes wet, chin trembling, opened her hands and un-coiled the bills. She held them, quivering, right up to his face.

The hangman took them, counted them out, studied them like he wasn't sure if they were play money or real. Mariah watched the hands that had tightened the rope around many a neck, around her own boy's neck, handle the money as ten-derly as he might a baby's fingers. He rolled it up and poked it back into her bodice. "I get paid good," he said. "Don't have no use for no nigger woman's shinplasters."

"You mean to tell me this money ain't worth nothing?" She'd sneaked and stole that money from the missus, she'd risked the whip for nothing?

"Won't say it's worthless. You might could eat off of it for three or four days."

"Where's my boy's body?!" Mariah screamed the words from somewhere deep inside her gut.

The hangman stood in the doorway and never even flinched. "This might surprise you in light of my profession," the hang-man said. "But I'm an honest man, and as such I'm obliged to tell you that the man hanged yesterday was a white man, white as I am." He pointed toward the woods, which were still dark. "Heard hounds early on this morning over beyond the Joyner place. That's enough to tell me the boy they was keeping there got loose."

Mariah couldn't believe it. "Oh, glory!" she shouted. She clenched her hands and bent over double. She sank down to her knees and sobbed. She held her tear-slicked face to the sky. "Oh, Jesus! Oh, glory!"

"Get up," the hangman said, after watching her carry on awhile. He grabbed both her wrists and pulled her up. She waited for him to tie up her wrists, shackle her feet. It was a white man's duty to turn in a runaway, and he seemed like a dutiful man. Mariah didn't care. She wasn't afraid of the beating she was bound to get. Her boy was free again. "Oh, Jesus!" she said again. "Oh, glory!"

"Go on," the hangman said. Mariah couldn't believe what she heard. "I said go on." Her mouth opened but nothing came out.

"You a good man, Master," she said, at last.

"I ain't a good man," the hangman said. "Just a satisfied one." He nodded toward the gallows. "Get my blood lust out regular, and get paid to do it. Now go on." He nodded at the bills poking up out of her bodice. "And don't be flashin' that around," he said. "No more than it's worth, they's still folks'll kill you for it."

So Mariah ran from the hanging place. She watched the sun and the stars and kept to a northerly direction, knowing that would be the direction Mosi, escaped, was sure to be headed. She believed she would find him. She walked on for days. Mostly she hugged the edge of the woods and ducked into them when she saw somebody. Sometimes she passed other slaves driving oxcarts, or on foot, and she'd ask them where she was. Right outside of Jesup, they might say, or on the road toward Savannah. "I'm looking for my boy Mosi," she'd say. "Anybody seen or heard tell of a boy named Mosi?" A lot of people had, but that didn't do Mariah a bit of good. Most everybody knew of a boy or a man named Mosi. Mosi meant firstborn.

Days and nights passed. Mariah was hungry. She remembered the hangman said she could buy a few days' worth of food with the money. She passed a store but was afraid to go in. What if the owner asked for a pass from her master, or asked whom she belonged to? What would she say? So Mariah made do on hickory nuts and cane roots and wild artichokes she gathered in the woods. She sneaked into a storehouse late one night and stole half a sack of cornmeal and a head of cabbage. That same night she huddled in the woods close to a stream. She used her flint rock and a little piece of steel to build a fire, then mixed up the cornmeal and water.

From the time she was a young girl working in the field, Mariah had always kept flint rock and steel in her pocket in case she up and stole away. She knew that way she could always make a fire to keep warm, could always cook a little food. All she would need was a pond or a creek and she would be able to survive for the next leg on the road toward freedom.

Mariah made a hoecake, wrapped it in cabbage leaves, and baked it in the ashes. She ate most of it and then washed her face and hands in the creek. Anything she'd ever had had gone right through her fingers just like that water. You couldn't hold on to a thing, not in this world. She made herself a bed out of moss, then lay down to rest. It was cool that night, and she left the fire going.

She awoke sometime later to shuffling sounds in the leaves nearby. A boy stood over the fire, looking down at her. The firelight made flutes and wedges of dark and light on his face. "Oh, glory!" she whispered, thinking she must be having a dream. Mariah sat up. "Mosi?"

She could see then that the boy was not Mosi. He was a mulatto boy. Mariah asked the boy to sit by the fire. His eyes were alive in the firelight, the way Mosi's had always been, as if he were full of motion even though he was sitting still, quivering from the inside the way runaways, terrified and desperate, always did. Mariah handed him what was left of her hoecake. He ate it with one bite, so Mariah got busy making him a fresh one. Even though he was not her son, the mother in her came alive. She moved around quickly, dipping her hands in the creek, then in the cornmeal, mixing it all up and rolling it in a cabbage leaf. Mariah was happy at that moment. It was good to have company, even though the boy wouldn't talk, even though she knew he would not be with her long. She handed him the hoecake when it was done, and he ate it, saying nothing. He just looked up at her between bites. When he was finished he nodded his thanks and disappeared into the woods.

The next morning, when Mariah arose from her moss bed, the embers had died in the fire, the sky was the color of meal, and the whole world seemed to have dulled overnight. The woods and the running creek were leached of color—everything was leached of color, except for her dress, which was red as oxblood.

She picked up the bloody kitchen knife that lay by her side. She tucked her hand into her bodice and found her money gone. Only then did she remember that the boy who had visited her the night before had come back, that she had awakened to find him towering over her. She recalled a moment of sudden fear, a brief struggle, then the dark.

From then on Mariah walked day and night. She passed by a squat house in the middle of a sandy field. She saw a little boy, five or six years old she judged, his head round as a ball, his hair like black wool, playing in a pile of sand not far from the front-porch steps. Mariah watched him, this ordinary little boy, as if she had never seen such a sight in all her days. She scooped him up in her arms and rubbed his head, circled her finger around his little ears. They were perfect as shells. She squeezed him so hard it made him cry. It frightened her that she frightened him. She tried to quiet him, held him up and pressed him to her face, clicked her tongue, tried to make him laugh. But she tried too hard, and that scared him all the more. He broke out into a loud, pitiful wail. The child's mother shot like a cannonball from the screen door. She screamed at Mariah, grabbed the baby, accused her of trying to steal him. Mariah held up her hands and shook her head to say she meant no harm, but the woman ran after her, the little boy wailing in her arms. The woman ran screaming at Mariah to stop haunting her. She screamed that Mariah had been there before, had tried to steal her child before, but Mariah had no memory of it. She did not mean to upset the child or frighten his mother.

Mariah, walking, sometimes wondered why she never seemed to get very far. Slowly, over time, the landscape changed. Fields wide as the world where cotton once grew became filled with houses. Many of the old sand roads were covered over with hard black tar, and shiny carriages flew down the roads without the aid of horses. Sometimes the people would stop and offer her a ride, and sometimes she would take them up on it. It was good to have a little company. She would exchange a few words with the driver, though Mariah and the driver could barely see each other's faces in the dark. A few miles up the road, near no particular landmark, Mariah would ask to be let out. She would thank the driver and walk on, realizing afresh that, no matter how far she walked or how many rides she took, she never seemed to get much farther along in her journey.

One night some lights caught her as she started to cross the road. She stepped back. The vehicle slowed to a stop. The driver leaned across the seat and opened the passenger door. Mariah slipped in, and they exchanged a few words. Mariah looked over at the driver and noticed a resemblance that was almost painful to recognize.

The boy drove on, his eyes moving back and forth between Mariah's face and the road. "Is there . . . some kind of a problem?" he asked.

She scooted next to him and grabbed his arm, sinking her fingers deep into it. Her eyes were on fire; she could feel it. No wonder he looked scared to death. The car swerved, but the boy was able to regain control just before it flew off the road, into a bog.

"Mosi?" Mariah asked.

"Say what? Who's Mosi?"

It was a name, like her own, that had a meaning. "Mosi," she said. "Firstborn."

The boy stepped hard on the brakes, pitching them both forward. He looked scared. Mariah didn't mean to scare him. "Look here, lady," he said, more breath than words, "I don't know who you're looking for, but I ain't him."

Alone on the road again, Mariah walked. She knew time kept passing like the wind at the tops of the pine trees, but she couldn't tell how much or how fast. Sometimes she saw some of the others driving oxen, guiding horses. Some seemed bent on a purpose, just as she was. Others seemed aimless, confused. Mariah just put one foot in front of the other and kept on walking. The road was white in the moonlight; it went on until the dark woods closed in around it, and Mariah knew it just kept on going after that.

BIRDS
of Silent Flight

What is left of the old rice plantation where the ghost of Miss Emmaline Elwood is sometimes seen straddles the Cape Fear River a few miles inland from the North Carolina coast. It has changed owners many times since the Civil War, and has been divided and sold off in parcels until only about five hundred of the original three thousand acres remain in one plot. That tract has been recently eyed by a developer, but thanks to the efforts of a group of environmentalists it has been bought by the state for a nature preserve. It will be a haven for wildlife, for the spindle-legged egrets, marsh hawks, ospreys, and ibises Miss Emmaline had loved so much. The preserve will also sustain more common birds, like the crows and grackles which once threatened the rice crop, and their cousins, the wicked, vandal blue jays. Miss Emmaline particularly despised the blue jays, because they rob other birds' nests and then fly off with the wind, accountable to none.

Marshland and thick maritime forest predominate. What was once the grand allée between giant live oak trees is now just a narrow sandy rift where deer leave footprints and an occasional alligator leaves a tail track. Union soldiers burned down most of the plantation buildings in 1864, so only the chimneys—not much more than vertical piles of rubble—stand like gravestones to mark where the Big House and the slave cabins once stood. The brick dovecote still stands tall like a medieval turret, though it is choked by scrub pines and palmetto palms. Until recently the roof still pressed down on the ruins of the old storehouse, and the Elwood family cemetery was hidden under prickly grasses and thick vines.

Once in a great while, solitary fishermen, many of whom

are descendants of Miss Emmaline's slaves, will claim to have seen Miss Emmaline floating face up in the lazy maze of tidal creeks that were once the plantation rice fields. Her face ripples in the water like the moon's reflection. Her hair waves like seaweed, and her dress fans out wide in the water like dark angel wings. Her eyes are always closed and she wears a short smile on her face, that smile all the dead wear, as if they've just made a most interesting discovery they know you'll stumble upon, too—and sooner than you think.

Whether or not the fishermen can be believed, this much is a matter of record: Miss Emmaline Elwood drowned herself one early spring afternoon in 1865. After the last two of her slaves left, she opened the floodgate of one of her family's rice fields, watched the water rise, lay down in it, and let the cool, brackish water cover her face. Two days later her sister, Bella, arriving from Richmond with her husband, had found Emmaline, arms outstretched, her face just under the surface of the water, so peaceful in death it was almost pretty, which was something she'd never been in life. They got the word out to everybody on the neighboring plantations, had the proper words said over her body, and buried her in the small family cemetery. When the news of Miss Emmaline's death got to her former slaves Ben and Delphia, Delphia shouted and grieved for days on end thinking that her and Ben's departure was the cause of Miss Emmaline's death.

But Emmaline's descent started many years before the war, when she was around twelve years old. She was the younger of two daughters, a reluctant belle, and a disappointment to both parents. The elder Elwood daughter, Bella, fair of face and full of grace, had made an acceptable, though not exceptional, marriage to a Virginia planter who had fewer acres and fewer slaves than the Elwoods. The marriage satisfied her parents that she would not be a spinster but did not do much to increase their financial or social fortunes. Mr. Elwood had only recently crossed the line from fair-to-middling farmer over to well-to-do planter, and Mrs. Elwood had been bequeathed an estate in South Carolina. But still the Elwoods' social standing, unlike their financial position, was not secure enough to satisfy Emmaline's mother, whose own mother had married beneath her, causing a break in the family's blue bloodlines. Emmaline's marriage to the right family name would seal the Elwoods' social position, would delight her mother and please her father. But she did not have the looks, charm, or social graces needed to compete with the lovely daughters of the local planter families, the Sneeds, the O'Reillys, and the Mortons.

At twelve years of age Emmaline cared not a thing about preening and fancywork and practicing at the pianoforte. But she loved traipsing through thickets, spying on wildlife with a pair of field spectacles, or sneaking off to go fishing at the creek with the slave boy Caleb, who always met her with a wide grin, a "Hey, Miss Emmaline," and unconditional acceptance. "Sure you purty, Miss Emmaline. You purty in a quiet kind of way. And you got things all them fancy women ain't never thought about. . . ."

Most of all, she loved feeding the pigeons, loved the predictability of it. She put out millet and they came. She kept the dovecote clean, they stayed. She always ran off into the woods when Delphia sent Ben to get the squabs. She wouldn't go down for dinner that night, knowing that the squabs would turn up fricasseed on a platter or stewed in a tureen on the supper table. Once she'd found out that the moist greasy birds she thought were wild game hens were really the offspring of her doves, she'd never eaten one, not one. She would have to be starving to death before she would eat one.

One spring day when white hominy clouds sailed high and fast across a blue sky, a day when even the usually silvery-gray river looked blue, she was happily scattering millet across the ground for the pigeons. She saw her mother and an aunt watching her from the mimosa tree where they were about to sit down for afternoon tea. This aunt was the kind who was always glad to see her, smiled with her whole face and waved with both her hands. Emmaline's mother, a naturally morose woman made bitter by unreached social aspirations and her husband's dalliances with slave girls, stared at her and stood straight as a fence post. Later, when Emmaline could not hear what they were saying over the chortling of the doves, knowing when they spoke softly she was often the subject of the discussion, she sneaked to a place behind the boxwood bushes where she could peep through the branches at them and hear all they said.

"Emmaline is barely twelve years old, Sally!" her aunt said, laughing, to Emmaline's mother. "She has a good four or five years before she is of marriageable age. Surely there is hope!"

"Hope?" her mother asked, with short, quick waves of her fan. "How can I ever hope to make a tea cake out of that hoecake?"

Emmaline had long suspected her mother's disdain, but she had never heard it said in so few, such hateful words. She slapped her hands over her ears, as if she could unhear what her mother had said, then turned and ran behind the dovecote, causing the doves covering the ground to scatter and fly away. She did not hear their startled chortling or the flutter of their wings. She ran through the back of the gardens, behind the wheelwright's shop, past the gin house to the slave street, and found Caleb on his way to the field. She'd been forbidden to play with Caleb, but she talked him into sneaking away. Together they went to fish at a creek deep in the woods, and didn't show their faces until suppertime. When they returned, Caleb got a whipping from the overseer, and Emmaline's mother sobbed while her father paced the floor, nearly frothing at the mouth, waving his arms like he was drowning in quicksand. "Cavorting with niggers! No decent man will ever cast his eyes in your direction!" He warned her: if he heard she'd merely looked up at Caleb from across the field, he would sell the boy for sure.

Emmaline stared back at them, her small pigeon eyes cold and hard as pebbles.

Two, three, four years went by, and Emmaline matured into a young woman with a notable resemblance to the doves she cared so much for. She had a small head, barely enough hair to fill up the snood at the nape of her neck, and narrow shoulders, which the broad, hooped dresses of the time made look all the narrower.

Unlike her doves she had poor eyesight but acute hearing, with which, over the years, she'd overheard snippets of condemnation. She had heard herself described as homely as a hoe handle. She had heard it said that, on her, the finest taffeta looked like twice-used casket lining. Not everybody was so unkind, but the words that stung the worst stayed in her mind the longest. At her own debut, Emmaline, in her olive drab dress and black snood, descended the staircase with all the splendor of a marsh duck and sat self-consciously on her debutante stool like she had a board nailed to her back. With the cruel words always ringing in her mind, surrounded as she was by lovely belles richly and colorfully dressed, Emmaline felt like a blot of liverwurst among the petit fours. With her mother standing by, pinning her eyes on Emmaline's every gesture, she trembled inside like a cockroach crawling among the finger sandwiches.

So she was surprised when Edwin Hampton, a not unhandsome, not uncharming young man whose father owned a cotton plantation at nearby Castle Hayne, paid her some attention. He asked her to dance the quadrille, the Virginia reel, and the tempest, one after the other, even though dancing with one partner in succession was considered rude to the other guests. Edwin was only distant kin to the prominent Hamptons, who owned plantations all over the Carolinas and Mississippi and were influential in government as well. But in that time and place the name *Hampton* was a kingly one, and Emmaline, for the first time in her life, was pleased to see the eyes of Miss Carolyn Sneed, from whom Edwin had been inseparable at the last fete, flash green. Emmaline also saw, for the first time in her life, looks of guarded approval in her parents' eyes.

After the ball, they spent some time with her over tea in the shade of the piazza, making sure she understood that to marry a Hampton would save her from spinsterhood, from ending up a shameful burden to her parents or her sister's family in Richmond. It would also secure the family's social standing. To encourage Edwin Hampton was no less than a sacred obligation.

Edwin visited often. They talked on the piazza, rode horses through the woods, walked along the live oak lane, observed Emmaline's doves circling and nesting at the dovecote, rowed along in the boat through the rice fields and down the silvery river. When weeks went by and Edwin still desired her company, Emmaline, for the first time, knew the heady rapture of being acknowledged, even—dare she think it?—desired by a man. She tried to ignore how often he worked the subject of Miss Caroline Sneed into their conversations.

Not until Edwin had asked for her hand in marriage did her father tell her he would give the new couple, for their wedding gift, the twenty-five-hundred-acre plantation on the Waccamaw River that had been bequeathed to Mrs. Elwood. No less than one hundred slaves came with it. It was a lavish gift, the kind only the wealthiest planters gave to their children. Emmaline quickly learned the Hamptons, including Edwin, had known this long before she did. Until that moment Emmaline had not been aware of how much she'd been flattered by Edwin Hampton's attentions, not until she learned their origins.

"Father," Emmaline said, her mild manner barely concealing the bitterness welling up in her, "you bribed him?"

"It is called a dowry," her father said. "You act as if it's a new idea, Emmaline. They have accepted it; you have accepted young Edwin's hand. And that's the end of it."

But that was not the end of it. That night Emmaline lay in bed under the mosquito net watching a mosquito caught in the white webbing. She got up and looked out the window. There in the moonlight, fishing from the dock at the creek behind the wheelwright's shop, sat Caleb, his profile silhouetted against the shining creek. She slipped down the big strong arms of the oak tree outside her window and ran down to him.

Caleb jumped and his eyes opened wide to see Emmaline gliding toward him, ghostlike in her white robe. He took off his hat and nodded. "Hey, Miss Emmaline!" She had seen him only rarely since her father had threatened to sell him, and always, like this time, under cover of night. She looked at him in a way she hadn't before. He cocked his head, smiled. "You doin' alright?" he asked, like he wasn't at all sure she was. She stepped forward and took his hand. "You look awful upset, Miss Emmaline. I do anything to help you?" To answer she kissed him on the forehead, both cheeks, his mouth. "Whoa, now, Miss Emmaline. What you doin'? If we was to get caught, your papa—"

"Father still lets you keep the keys to the rice barn, doesn't he, Caleb?" He nodded. She took his hand and led him there. They met at the rice barn on several nights after their first night together. It went on for weeks, well into the early preparations for the wedding.

Emmaline began to show, and she knew she would soon have no choice but to tell. Her face had grown fuller, her upper arms fatter. But Emmaline had always been gaunt, and her mother and sister, Bella, who was visiting to help with the wedding, remarked that her filling out was a good thing. The full-skirted dresses of the time hid many imperfections and improprieties, so it was not until the first fitting for her wedding gown that her condition could not be denied. Her mother shrieked like a shore bird at the sight of Emmaline's rounded belly pushing out from her chemise. "Oh, Emmaline, no!" She sank on the settee, steadied herself there, then let her face crumple. Bella, with whom Emmaline had already shared her situation, stood by, her face pained. "Oh, Emmaline, tell me this is not so!" her mother said. "Does Edwin know about it? Do the Hamptons know?"

"It is not Edwin Hampton's," Emmaline announced.

Her mother, face stricken, slowly rose up from the settee; Bella, afraid her mother would fall, held onto her. "Then whose could it be?"

"I don't know," Emmaline replied. Her mother's mouth fell open; she slapped Emmaline hard across the face, then fell back on the settee and dissolved into sobs, wails, and dry heaves. Delphia ran into the drawing room with smelling salts, and the house girls stood in the doorway, wild-eyed and fidgety. At the stables and the shops within earshot of Mrs. Elwood's wails, work stopped for a full minute and everybody looked up.

Emmaline's mother declared she was glad Mr. Elwood was in Savannah on business and would not be back for two weeks. That way maybe she would die before he came back and she had to give him such despicable news. For days afterward Mrs. Elwood stayed in her room, mumbling, sobbing, screaming they were all ruined, declaring she was ready to die. Following her tirades she would sleep for hours. Bella and Delphia took Mrs. Elwood tea, tried to make her eat, tried to console her, but they failed to. The house girls all walked with their heads lowered. The house, the work yard, even the fields were abuzz with the news of Miss Emmaline's expecting. They were all afraid for Caleb, of what Master Elwood would do when he found out, for, no matter if Miss Emmaline told it or not, they had seen her and Caleb together.

When news reached the Hamptons, Edwin sent Emmaline a letter expressing his gratitude that "circumstances allowed me to discover early this weakness in your character which would have been fatal to any good fortune Providence had predestined for us." Visitors from neighboring plantations entered the foyer with lowered eyes and voices, as if calling on a house where death itself had visited. It was social death for certain, because, even though Emmaline did not admit to it, the suspicion spread quickly that she was with child by a slave boy.

Only Emmaline's sister would greet the visitors. She offered the curious guests tea, and they took it with eyes shining, darting. They were excited over the deliciousness of the scandal, not daring to ask direct questions, but hoping some snippet might slip out in normal conversation. It was a most unfortunate, yet delectable, development, as rich as duck liver pâté, sweet as saltwater taffy, too good not to whisper about. Bella returned to Richmond before their father came home, knowing she could not withstand the chest-beating and hair-tearing that was sure to follow.

When Mr. Elwood received the news he slumped in his wing chair, seething quietly, his face in his hands. "Who is responsible?" he asked. "Who?" No answer. Both Emmaline and her mother were afraid to speak. "Who? Young Edwin, I presume?"

"No, Father," Emmaline said.

"Then who?" No answer. "Speak!"

"I believe," her mother said, whimpering, "I am quite sure it is your plowboy, Caleb."

His eyes scorched Emmaline's face.

Emmaline knew that when her father wanted to get rid of troublesome slaves, he sold them to a merchant in Wilmington known for his brutality. So, for the first time in her life, Emmaline fell down at her father's knees and wailed. "It was not Caleb, Father! I swear it! Oh, please don't sell him, Father, please!"

Her father looked at his sobbing daughter, his eyes ablaze. Then he laid one hand stiffly on her head. "Alright, Emmaline," he said, in an eerily composed voice she had never heard before. "You have my word. I will not sell Caleb."

Her father was as good as his word: he did not sell Caleb. But that night a shot rang out, and that was the last anybody ever saw of Caleb. Emmaline cried so long and so hard that Delphia fussed over her and rarely left her side, fearful she would lose the baby.

In the intervening months Emmaline's father stayed in the fields, or in Wilmington, or wherever business took him. Her mother wore shame on her face; it weighed on her shoulders. Emmaline and her mother passed each other in the darkened hallways like ghosts, sat across from each other in the drawing room, ate meals at opposite ends of the table, in silence.

"Will you punish me forever, Mother?" Emmaline asked one day, in her ninth month.

"It is not my place to punish you, Emmaline." Her mother looked up from her plate and leaned forward. Her eyes burned with wicked certainty. "Be assured Providence will see to that."

Her mother refused to enter the room while Emmaline was in labor. It was Delphia, not her mother, who held her hands, wiped her forehead, listened to her screams. The child was small, sickly, and, though she had Caleb's features and coarse hair, she was pale of hue. When Delphia had washed the baby and laid her in Emmaline's arms, she said, "Look here! She like a little lemon!" Emmaline chose to call her Lemon. Her mother scoffed, then told her to call the child whatever she wished; the child was not long for that house, anyway.

One night Emmaline awoke and caught her mother looking over the crib, watching Lemon with a look in her eyes that was far from grandmotherly. That Lemon was her own blood would not matter to Mrs. Elwood. Lemon was slave stock and good for sale. To be rid of her would rid the household of shame, the shame of having a daughter who birthed yellow babies and a husband who had sired them. Selling Lemon would be as good for the house as the big cleaning and airing that Delphia directed every March.

So from that day on Emmaline kept Lemon with her night and day. From infancy Lemon slept in Emmaline's bed and never left her side. Lemon was like a doll Emmaline had never outgrown, would not let out of her sight, could not leave the house without. Only when her mother was visiting Bella in Richmond, and was gone for weeks at a time, did Emmaline allow Lemon the run of the plantation. She thought the slaves might grow to resent Lemon's place of privilege, so she let her play with the slave children in the work yard where their mothers did laundry, let her dip her hand into the trough and scoop up the milk-sopped bread that the slave children ate. She let her join them for the little games of tag they played between the big iron laundry kettles, and games of hide-and-seek all over the plantation.

At thirteen years of age Lemon had grown into a young girl, all arms and legs, full of motion. "Can't you be still a minute?" Emmaline would ask her as they sat cross-legged on the bed while Emmaline tried to braid Lemon's hair into long, yellow-hued ropes. They tended the dovecote together. They didn't act or look a thing like mother and daughter. Many times Emmaline had looked at Lemon and wondered if this was the wages of her sin. She could not have hoped for a finer gift if she had led the virtuous life of a nun.

In the winter of 1860, after years of steady decline, Emmaline's mother died of country fever. Then came the war and all the suffering and deprivation it caused. Her father went off to fight, as did the overseer, Edwin Hampton, and nearly every other white man she knew. Emmaline became worn and ragged from managing the house, the rice crop, and the slaves, which she would have been unable to do without the wise and loyal Ben and Delphia.

But those bad days were good days for Lemon. She was free of the tyranny of Emmaline's mother, she had the run of the plantation, she played with the slave children whose mothers worked the field, she helped Delphia in the kitchen. She took over the care of the dovecote, she roamed the grounds exploring, on horseback, on foot. She was giddy with her newfound freedom. Emmaline stayed busy trying to keep the place limping along.

By the time her father had died of typhoid at Malvern Hill, Emmaline, with the help of Ben and the other field hands, had learned enough to save the rice crop and look ahead to the next one. Ben taught her to see that the rice was well clayed before the seeds were sown in the watery fields. Times got tougher by the week, but starvation was some distance away. They still had cowpeas, rice, fish in the streams, wild game in the woods, and thirty acres of white pine that Emmaline could sell for lumber.

That November, Emmaline got word that somebody was cutting and stealing the pine, and she and Ben picked a day to go and confront the thief and try to get amends. Lemon begged to go, but Emmaline wouldn't let her. There was a lot of business to do that day. They had to see that the rice was properly clayed in the back fields, too.

On the way back in the early evening they heard the earth thunder with horse hooves. Shouts carried across the marsh. They smelled smoke. Ben slapped the oars hard in the water, and a few minutes later they could see smoke swirling like a black funnel cloud above the Big House. Flames shot up the chimney and licked around the front columns; a section of roof waffled, came loose, and sailed away into the woods.

In front of the house Delphia and the house girls, choking in the smoke, scrambled to keep the pigs and chickens from running away into the woods, knowing that what livestock they had left would soon be all that stood between them and starvation.

"Where's Lemon?! Where's Lemon?!" Emmaline leapt toward the burning, crumbling porch, and it took Ben and Delphia both to hold her back. "Oh no, Missus, she ain't in there!

"She ain't none of them places, either!" Delphia cried out when Emmaline's eyes flashed wildly from the burning loom house to the stables, the cabins.

Emmaline turned her eyes on them. Sweat ran down their faces; fire danced in their eyes. "How do you know? Tell me how you know that!"

Most of what happened she learned afterwards. The Union soldiers had taken anything they could carry or haul behind them on horseback, everything from the hams in the smokehouse and the silver they found hidden in the fireplace to as many cows and horses as they could tow. Before they left, the officer looked around and said, "You boys see anything else you want?" One of them had eyed Lemon, who was huddled under a tree with Delphia and the house girls, and said, "I'll have me that yellow girl, sir. Always did want me a yellow girl." The officer nodded. They had pulled Lemon from Delphia's clutches and had carried her off, despite Delphia screaming, "Don't take our baby! Sweet Jesus, don't let them take our baby!" and all of Lemon's screaming, kicking, and crying. The soldier threw her on a horse and ran away with her. The other devils in blue coats set fire to the Big House, the workshops, the cabins, the stable.

"But Miss Lemon was always crafty, Miss Emmaline!" Delphia cried out, grabbing Emmaline by the shoulders. "Might be she got loose, is making her way back already!"

Emmaline looked around at what was left to her: burning house and buildings, a few slaves who could leave her now anytime they wanted to, and one terrified, buck-jumping horse, which one of the field hands had roped and was wrestling with to keep it from bolting. That one horse, she figured, had been left to her for a reason. Right then that one horse was worth more to her than anything she had ever owned. "Saddle him up," she told Ben, "and be quick about it."

"Oh, Miss Emmaline!" Delphia cried, squeezing Emmaline's fingers. "You can't catch up with them Yankees!"

"I know it," Emmaline said.

"You a fool to try, Miss Emmaline," Ben said.

"I know that too."

Emmaline rode northward for three days over every back road, calling out for Lemon, crying out for her, like a drover for his lost sheep. Everywhere the Big Houses had been burned: Kingwood, Argyle, Mimosa. At the Mimosa plantation only the chimney and the foundation remained. Everywhere in the wake of the Northern soldiers' retreat was smoke, rubble, destruction. She tried not to think of what might be ahead for Lemon, of what might have befallen her already. It was known that the soldiers did more than trash and plunder; they raped and tortured as well.

Whatever had happened to Lemon, Emmaline believed she would see her again. She was crafty, as Delphia had said, and she would come back. She would free herself from the Yankee soldier. No matter how far north he took her, no matter how long she was gone, one day she'd find her way across mountains, rivers. She'd find her way back home. Believing this, having to believe it, Emmaline, weary and starving, was able to turn tail and go back to the plantation and salvage what she could.

When she got back she found most of her slaves gone. They'd headed inland, where some planter was doling out acres to the freedmen in exchange for half their yield of cotton. Only Ben and Delphia remained, mainly out of pity for her. They promised to stay with Emmaline until the middle of March to help her with the first rice planting. Twice she received letters from Bella asking her to come stay with her in Richmond, but Emmaline wrote back that she had learned early on what a shameful thing it is to be a burden on a family member. And she must be there to greet Lemon on her return.

Emmaline, Ben, and Delphia spent the winter hovelled together in what was left of the rice barn. They lived off what rice was left, dried cowpeas, and fish they caught in the creeks. By early spring there was nothing much left to eat but the fish in the creeks, and the smell of it sickened them. In March Ben and Delphia helped her plant a small crop of rice. One good crop of rice meant hope for another, bigger one, and another after that. A good crop of rice meant a measure of prosperity, the means to rebuild some of what she'd had. When Lemon returned she'd have a place to call home.

Ben warned her she couldn't expect to keep it going without some hands to help her out. "I got hands, don't I? Yours and Delphia's," Emmaline said. Ben shook his head and warned her again they were there on borrowed time.

One warm March day Ben and Delphia stood by the gate, each holding one rice seed bag half filled with something—whatever they'd been able to salvage from their cabins, she guessed. Ben carried the musket he'd had with them that day in the boat, the day the Yankees had come. Delphia was crying. "Stayed as long as we could, Miss Emmaline," Ben said.

"You all can't leave me."

"We looked after you a long time, Miss Emmaline, but we got to look out for Ben and Delphia now."

"Where will you go?"

"Man up near Chinquapin promised us some acres, some hogs, a mule."

"I can't make a promise like that, but if you all stay with me, you can have all the rice you can eat when it comes in. Things will get better." Ben looked over her shoulder at the rice fields and shook his head. She turned to see what he was looking at.

A great black cloud of crows, cackling and cawing, swarmed over the field and alighted on it. They made the rice fields as dark as black water in a swamp. There had been several days of westerly winds, and the fields were nearly dry. Not enough water had come in with the tide, and the rice seed was as exposed as if it had been laid out for the blackbirds to feed on. Ben aimed the musket and fired it; the crows scattered, but they settled in the trees beyond the marsh, waiting to come back. "Ain't likely to be much yield this go-round, Missus. Not unless you fire every time them crows settle. Won't take long before they won't pay it no mind." He handed the musket to her. "You likely to need this more than us, Miss Emmaline."

"Y'all can't leave me!" she said again while Ben slung the rice sack over his back and they started down the road. Ben hung his head, and Delphia sobbed. "If you go, it'll be like they've taken everything I ever had! You'll be back!" she cried, and she was right.

They did come back within the year, and some of their descendants live nearby wherever development has not rooted them out.

Emmaline, alone with her ruins, stood and watched Ben and Delphia diminish as they walked down the road. Some days passed, and Emmaline ate the last of the rice and the last jar of salt pickles they'd salvaged from the Big House. Fish now made her sick. She could not hold it down. She visited the dovecote, thinking she would surely pick apart a fat squab now. But she had no millet, so even the doves who circled the tower wouldn't stay long. She wondered if maybe there was some millet in the old storehouse; Ben used to keep it there years before the rice barn was built, but surely it would be old and molded by now. Still, that got her thinking about the storehouse, how Delphia wouldn't go there because she was petrified of rats. Ben had talked of the day he might have to go shoot the rats so they'd have meat to eat, and both Delphia and Emmaline had nearly gagged at the thought of it. But now, Emmaline thought, a rat roasted over the fire might not taste so bad.

So she went through the woods to the storehouse. It was a little ways from the other plantation buildings and, probably for that reason, had escaped the Yankee soldiers' notice. Yet, of all the buildings the soldiers might have burned, it was the one that would have been the easiest to lose. It was an old house, already on the grounds when Mr. Elwood established the plantation, and though they called it the storehouse it was really nothing more than a depository of old junk. Nobody went there, except Ben. The door hung open. Armed with the musket and every intention of finding herself a rat, she entered.

The storehouse smelled like iron, leather, and faintly, very faintly, of dead rats, a smell that had once nauseated her, but did not now. She heard them scuttling; she could almost see them hiding, rising on hind legs, their pink toes twiddling, their noses twitching, curious about who had invaded their domain. She walked behind the barrels of bent nails that the blacksmith had stored there decades ago, a big iron washtub rusted through, piles of worn saddles and bridles, broken fish-nets, piles of lumber. She had to watch her step on the rotting floors. She walked around rusted iron bedsteads, old mattress ticks. She looked in an empty cedar wardrobe and an old steamer trunk, which was empty too, except for a wad of moth-eaten old blanket and a smell that threw her backwards. Now, how many rats would it take to make a smell that strong? Under the blanket she found a pile of yellow ropes with a pale face attached to it. Parched skin stretched over bone.

Will you punish me forever, Mother?

Providence will see to that.

Emmaline opened her mouth, but not a sound came out, not that she could hear. Her head felt like it was filled with cotton. Her mind circled and circled the thing in the trunk but wouldn't alight on it. She thought instead of what must have been the quick escape from the Yankee soldiers, the terrified flight through the woods, the choice to hide here in the one building not on fire that night, of the terror when the trunk snapped shut and wouldn't open from the inside. The fingers, she could see, had been worn down almost to the bone.

And where were the ones who had made this happen? Gone, those with the blue coats, gone like flocks of noisy, greedy, hateful blue jays dispersed over the countryside. She looked up and straight ahead. A small round window was cut into the wall behind the trunk, and through it she watched the flock of crows once again covering the newly planted rice.

The rice was everything now; it was the last of the last. So she ran to protect it. She couldn't hear the sound of her feet thudding through the woods and across the yard to the rice fields. She couldn't hear the sound of the gunshot when she fired into the flock, or the flutter and the wing beat of the thousand crows, those scavengers who had come right out of the sky to undo all she'd done, to take the last of what was hers and then just fly away with it, gone like an arrow shot across the sky. She didn't hear her sister, Bella, scream when they found her two days later. She had already opened the floodgate and let it fill the rice field. She was already floating faceup in the water, her hair like seaweed, her dress spread wide like angel wings, just as she sometimes appears, so they say, even to this day.

The nature preserve which was once the Elwood rice plantation is visited mostly by naturalists interested in the diverse wildlife. In the summer months, only the tittering, screeching, and squawking of birds breaks up the constant insectival hum. In the winter months the quiet roars like a shell held to the ear.

The workers who prepared the preserve for the public disrupted the thick forest cover only to cut a few crude trails and install some trash bins. A narrow, nature-friendly path has been cut out leading to the dovecote, where doves, likely descended from Miss Emmaline's, still circle and alight, still poke their small heads into the nesting holes and look around curious and serious, as if they know it is their ancestral home. The workers cleared similar paths to the chimneys which mark where the Big House and the slave cabins once stood.

They dismantled the old storehouse, but not before they looked it over inside and out to see if there was anything worth preserving—some artifact or implement that might suggest how the people of that place and time had lived. They trimmed back the wild growth from the graves at the Elwood family graveyard, and they put up a modest stone, with no name on it, over a grave they had just recently filled.

The Dressmaker's MANNEQUIN

On a cobblestone backstreet in New Orleans, in a dusky alcove of a shop full of antiques and curios and vintage clothing, under a high shelf where perched an antique jester doll with wide-open eyes and fixed, raised eyebrows, stood a dressmaker's mannequin.

She was made of wood aged dark and rough as a whiskey barrel; she had no head, no arms, and no legs. She had been built more than a century and a half ago to be the seamstress's model for a young plantation belle. She therefore had a young woman's build—bosom rounded like two young honeydew melons, a long narrow waist like a wasp's, and hips slender as a newt's. Two screws and a piece of rusted scrap metal barely held together the unsightly gap between her hips and torso; termites had nibbled ridges and worms had bored holes all over her surface, and she was warped in places from decades of Louisiana delta dampness. Though the mannequin had forborne years of mishandling and misuse, she had maintained a young Victorian lady's gentle, refined sensibilities. But now that the shopkeeper had removed her from her prominent position in his display window and had relegated her to the rear of the shop, she could barely corset her seething, combustible rage.

The shopkeeper, Monsieur Louie Laveau, a tall man around thirty years old with ears, hands, and feet too big for his boney frame, was given to wild gesticulations and shameless displays of emotion. The mannequin loved him, but the little jester, a spiteful creature who had sat spread-eagle in his harlequin jumpsuit on that shelf for years, despised Monsieur Laveau, had declared him a forked-tongued, blithering, spasmodic idiot. "'I marvel your ladyship takes delight in such a barren rascal,'" the jester had said, quoting Shakespeare in a low, guttural, vaguely British accent.

But the wooden mannequin had loved Monsieur Laveau from the day he had rescued her from a city Dumpster. She loved him with a blazing passion that she knew was fated never to be consummated, or even expressed.

For a year the mannequin had been the undisputed darling of Laveau's shop. Except for the rolltop desk where he did his paperwork, she was the one large item that was clearly marked NOT FOR SALE. Dressed in vintage clothing from different eras, she had stood proudly on her wooden three-legged stand in the shop window. There she served as the centerpiece of one or the other of Monsieur Laveau's constantly changing nostalgic vignettes, for which he had been featured in magazines, had won accolades and awards. She had posed as a young plantation belle sitting primly in a gazebo, as an aproned young housewife cooking at a wood-stove, as a young mother sitting by a Christmas tree with little children and presents scattered at her feet, as a femme fatale of the 1930s reclining on a fainting couch, and, most recently, as a Victorian bride in a full-skirted, crème-and-rose brocade bridal gown.

But the gown had been sold, and now the mannequin, stripped of her finery, stood naked and unadorned. The shop window which had been her stage was empty, was undergoing renovation, and the mannequin was afraid she might not be restored to her queenly position in the window, that she might be permanently relegated to that alcove next to the broom closet, under the shelf where that obnoxious jester perched. But the thing she feared worst of all was that Monsieur Laveau would decide to put her up for sale. The mannequin did not want to be sold. She'd rather be stored inside the broom closet than be sold. She'd rather be sawed into quarters, or planed for paper, or ground into sawdust. She feared being sold more than she feared the blow of an ax or slow disintegration by termites, or being reduced to ashes by fire. To be sold meant to be thrust again into the unknown. It might mean days in Dumpsters, decades in damp warehouses. But worst of all, to be sold meant eternal separation from her beloved Monsieur Louie Laveau.

One day shortly after her demotion, two historical society matrons, white haired and well coiffured, stepped into the shop. "Look, there's an old-fashioned dressmaker's form," one of them said. "I last saw one of those in my grandmother's attic."

The woman who had spoken tapped the mannequin's torso with her cane. The other looked the mannequin over through bifocals dropped halfway down her nose. "My land, she certainly has been through a lot, hasn't she? You can certainly tell she's not a reproduction."

"Wouldn't she look clever in the historical society's museum?" the woman with the cane said. "There's plenty of money in the budget this year." She reached into her purse for a tape measure, and together the two women measured the mannequin from shoulder to hip. "Five feet even from the floor. She'd be just the thing to replace that fan palm that died." They asked Monsieur Laveau if she was for sale.

The mannequin was terrified.

"Oh!" Monsieur Laveau slapped his forehead. "No, mesdames! Not for sale!"

The mannequin inwardly beamed.

"Looks like she was made after a young woman," the lady with the cane said as they walked away, "but I bet she's older than Methuselah."

"Oh yes! Wouldn't you just love to know her history?" her friend replied.

The mannequin did indeed have a history. She had served for three decades as a seamstress's model in the sewing room of a southern Louisiana plantation house. She had been useful there, as necessary to the successful running of the Big House as the maids, the laundresses, the cooks, and the little ones who fanned flies off the young missus as she ate her dinner.

The mannequin owed her existence, such as it was, to old Uncle Keg, the plantation carpenter. Uncle Keg had one good brown eye; the other eye was blind, and blue as indigo. His hair and beard were like cotton before it was ginned; his face was brown and shriveled like an old dried pecan, and he looked—some of the slaves said he was—older than God. He made all the caskets the year so many died of malaria, mumbling all the while he planed and sanded the wood, as if he were conferring with the dead over the specifications.

In 1831 Uncle Keg made the mannequin in the size and shape of the young missus, so the seamstress at the Big House could use her wooden form to make the young woman's clothes. Uncle Keg knew there were spirits in every rock, river, and tree. Just like the master's boy who had hunted alligators for no better reason than he happened to know where all the big alligators lived, Uncle Keg, knowing what he knew, couldn't help but go out every now and again to catch a spirit.

He made the mannequin out of a virgin cypress, that lordly tree of swamps and bayous. The mannequin had only the dimmest recollection of her stately, moss-draped limbs and deeply rutted trunk, of herself as a tree reflected in eerie black water. She remembered the first sharp blow of the ax and the long fall to the soggy ground, but the thought was as murky as the water had been, only half-remembered, like a child's memory of its birth. Dim too were her recollections of all that happened later—she was milled, planed, routed, and shaped, and Uncle Keg sanded her chocolate-hued wood to a silky finish and applied coat after coat of protective oil stain. But she did remember hours and hours of hemmings, fittings, and refittings as she stood in front of the floor-length mirror in the plantation sewing room. And she well remembered the young missus, now long, long dead.

The young missus sometimes surprised the mannequin and the seamstress by beaming into the sewing room like sunshine, to try on her clothes and talk about her troubles and the loves of her life. The young missus was effervescent as a mineral spring, all heart and nerves, and the mannequin, made in the image of the young missus, hung on her every word and gesture and, in her own limited way, became those things too. How few and far between were those who ever knew she had feelings.

"She a real girl, Mama?" the seamstress's little daughter asked one time, looking up at the mannequin from the floor, where she toddled around while the seamstress pinned the hem of a chemise. She was a little pigtailed girl with a lot of gum showing when she smiled. "Uncle Keg say she is."

"No, she ain't no real girl!" the seamstress said, her mouth bristling with pins. "Ain't no more'n a stick o' wood!"

The mannequin felt the sting of those words like a blow from an ax.

"I believe she a real girl," the little girl said. "If she had a head, she could talk."

After the War Between the States the family abandoned the house, and the mannequin had languished in the attic for two decades, slumped against the wall as if she had been back-handed by a cruel master whose orders she had disobeyed or whose romantic attentions she had rebuffed. She was covered up in dust and cobwebs thick as a quilt, in a rat's jungle of junk. The Big House passed from one new owner to the next.

The mannequin had been packed in boxes and shipped, strapped to the luggage racks of cars, and hauled up and down the East Coast. She had been displayed in store corners and storefronts from Atlanta to Chicago to New York; she had been a part of the decor in city loft apartments, in restaurants and bars. When her last owner died she had lain on her back for years in his dank basement, until his heirs had gotten around to clearing away and junking its contents, which included her.

She had counted it as her good fortune that after such a hard time she ended up in a Dumpster not far from Monsieur Laveau's shop. Monsieur Laveau had been rummaging through the Dumpster, as he did from time to time, looking for lost treasures, when he found her. "Ah! *Mais oui!*" he said when he saw her near the top of the Dumpster, under rain-sodden paper sacks of magazines and a pink, quilted housecoat and bags of garbage. How gallantly he had rescued her, his arm crooked around her waist as he lifted her out, how like the lover on the cover of a racy romance novel!

She was instantly smitten. "Had a bad time of it, *jeune fille*?"

he had said as he carried her down the street, tenderly cupped in his arms. He had carried her into his shop in a grand manner, as he might have carried a bride across the threshold. He had dressed her that first day in a nineteenth-century lady's shirtwaist and street skirt—clothes so much like the ones she had once modeled for the young missus—and had set her up in the storefront window. She had felt she had come home at last after a long and terrible journey.

From that day on she had modeled the vintage clothing he acquired from estate sales and other venues, anything that fit her, which was most things: capes, collarettes, walking skirts, shirtwaists, and automobile coats, most from that era she remembered so well. So the mannequin spent many pleasant days and nights as the star of Monsieur Laveau's storefront scenes. At Christmas she stood by an old-fashioned, gas-lit lamppost—dressed in a long coat and fur muffler, as if she were ready to walk out and go caroling. Other times she wore a long, full-skirted silk dress and "played" a minuet at an old clavichord he had acquired. During Mardi Gras she had sat on a throne, resplendent in the gown and robe worn by the Mardi Gras queen of 1898.

Months had passed and contentment had settled over the mannequin. Of all the places she'd been stored or displayed, none had matched Monsieur Laveau's shop window. She delighted in the yellow jasmine and the lavender wisteria that catapulted down the brick walls and wrought-iron fences at the inn across the street. How she loved the energy of Christmas, New Year's, the wonderful insanity of Mardi Gras! The motley parade of customers who walked by her window! The down-and-out saxophonist who would play his sweet, sad music for her right outside the shop, then tap on the window, look up at her, and say, "We pass good time, yeah, *chéri*?" How she had reveled in the carnival spirit which prevailed all year long in this city, where it was understood that everything was—as the mannequin most certainly was—more than it seemed to the naked eye! But her happiness at all times hung on the praises that Monsieur Laveau heaped upon her.

That was no secret to the Harlequin, who could read her

every thought and loved to taunt her. Sometimes, late at night, when the caterwauling at the bars up the street had died down and it was so quiet she could hear the rats skittering in the darkened corners, when the shop lay in the crossed shadows made by the streetlights outside, there would be stirrings of life in the shop. The ivory ball circled in the rotating wheel of the antique roulette table; on the walls the feathered masks stirred in the air. At such times and in such places, so the mannequin had learned from much experience, a secret communion goes on that only occurs between seemingly mute, insensate things.

One day, Monsieur Laveau spent a good half hour making adjustments in the window display, where the mannequin, dressed in the everyday attire of a nineteenth-century young woman, sat riding an old unicycle he had acquired just the day before. He stood back for an overview, his hands clasped in midair. "Ah! *Jeune fille!*" he said, delighted. "What a find you were!"

Late that night the mannequin, perched on the unicycle, faced out the front window toward the street. She was stage-lit by the streetlight outside. The darkened shop lay behind her. It was quiet. Even the music from the bar up the street had died down. The jester broke the silence.

"Don't flatter yourself you're special," the jester grumbled from his place on the shelf.

"Why, I don't know what you mean!" she said.

"Just because you get the front window and he blows sweet nothings your way, doesn't mean he cares a fig for you. The day something else catches his eye you'll be gone—poof!—kindling for a fire."

"That's not true!" she said. "That's not true!" But the seed of doubt had been planted. What if it was true? She had heard it said that a jester speaks the truth no one else will.

"That's right!" the jester whispered, reading her thoughts. "You're nothing to him but a cheap tailor's dummy!"

"And you, sir," she shot back, angry, but proud of her quip, "are—quite literally—a FOOL!"

"'A fool knows his foolishness is wise,'" the jester said.

"Cheap dummy!" screeched the stuffed scarlet macaw in the antique birdcage. "A fool! A fool!"

No! the mannequin thought. She had not been a fool! Monsieur Laveau had declared his affection for her on many occasions!

She remembered the time when he had placed her in a chair at a vanity table covered with a lace runner and old French perfume bottles, silver combs, and brushes. Her headless upper body was framed in the mirror, topped by the wide tailored yoke of the shirtwaist she wore. Monsieur Laveau had stood behind her, held her by the shoulders, and with genuine affection in his voice he had said, "There now, *jeune fille*! Aren't we a picture!"

She remembered the time he had positioned her on an old fainting couch he'd recently brought to the shop, had draped about her an old bolt of rich red brocade and placed a champagne glass on the table beside her. "Well now, aren't you the femme fatale!" Monsieur Laveau had said. Was that not passion she had perceived burning in his eyes?

"'Twas merely dust burning his eyes, causing him to squint!" the jester, who could read her every thought, said.

"Oh! You—!"

"There was the wooden Indian maid in the window before you," the jester said, grimly, "and before her a plaster of paris statue of Venus, the goddess of love and beauty—the epitome, she was, of style and grace. He adored her, but he got rid of her, even her."

The mannequin tried not to listen. She remembered the day Monsieur brought to her, draped over his arm, the shimmery crème-and-rose brocade bridal gown. Miraculously, it had fit her like a glove, and the mannequin, perhaps childishly, thought the coincidence was significant, thought perhaps there was some hope that. . . .

Monsieur Laveau had held her by the waist and stood back from her as if he were ready to sweep her across a ballroom. "Ah, *jeune fille*!" he had said, "Don't you cut a lovely figure!" And then, and then . . . he had planted a kiss in the air right where her head would be if she had one. "Mmmmwaa!" The sound erupted from his pursed lips. *"Je t'aime!"* he had said. Yes! Yes! He had declared his love!

"'She is mad,'" the jester growled, "'who trusts in the tameness of a wolf.'"

Not long after Monsieur Laveau's declaration of love, the lovely gown was sold. And then Monsieur Laveau had moved her, with no more ceremony than he would move an empty crate, to the alcove where she now stood, under the very shelf where sat the obnoxious—and omniscient—jester.

Now each day the workmen came. The shop window and the display area began to take shape. They busily repainted the trim at the window panes, replaced cracked glass, and lined the floor of the stagelike space with rich red velvet.

Monsieur Laveau left on a buying trip. The mannequin was beside herself with worry that she would be sold before he returned, that she would never see him again. She was worried about who would replace her in the display window and, thereby, in his affections. In the long days and evenings that followed, the out-of-synch tick-tick, tock-tick, tick-tock-tock of the antique French clocks marked the hours as they clipped by like a lame horse unsure of its footing.

"He loves you, he loves you not," the jester mocked in a high-pitched voice. "He loves you, he loves you . . . not!"

Meanwhile, the tiny, shuffling, pearl-haired woman who was minding the shop in his absence talked to the dealers and customers who called wanting to speak to Laveau. "He'll be away until next week," she would say. The mannequin heard her tell one customer, "Oh, I hear he's having a marvelous time, an unusually marvelous time! Yes, he sounds awfully excited about something. Well, now, I don't know about that. You know he's always sworn he'd stay a bachelor, but who can tell? He did say he made an acquisition he is very excited about. Who can guess what it is?"

That something was, Monsieur Laveau announced when he came back, the greatest acquisition of his career—an entire collection of party dresses, ball gowns, and chemises from the 1920s and 1930s, from the estate of a woman whose mother was Louise Moore, the famous film actress from that era. All throughout the day Monsieur Laveau loped from the street into the shop carrying armloads of shimmering dresses. Many were white and fringed with silver, like angel garb, others were brilliant jewel-toned chiffon flapper dresses with hand-kerchief hemlines, and there were some of exquisite crème silk decorated with hand-sewn seed pearls. When all the dresses and hats were hung and the vintage wigs placed on Styro-foam heads along the fireplace mantel, Monsieur Laveau stood in the middle of the shop, his feet together and his arms outstretched. The shop was a shimmering, glimmering artist's palette of color, an extravagance of glamour and style. "Ah! *Magnifique!*" he said.

The mannequin was beside herself with delight, for she thought she would be the one to wear these glorious garments in the newly renovated display window. Then later that same day a courier carried into the shop a bundle thickly bound in bubble wrap. Monsieur Laveau peeled the plastic aside, slowly, as if unwrapping a mummy that the slightest pull of the plastic could easily crumble. The figure that emerged looked nothing like a mummy.

It looked more like a perfectly preserved corpse, though far lovelier. It was a wax mannequin. She had a lovely head, pale and polished like a cameo and tilted coquettishly to the side. She had eyes, lashes, a lovely aquiline nose, and painted lips pinched like a bow. Her body, with just a suggestion of breasts and buttocks, was the perfect replica of a 1920s flapper. She posed with her knees slightly bent, long-nailed fingers out to the side as if she had been frozen while dancing the Charleston.

Monsieur Laveau circled the wax mannequin, his eyes scanning her from head to toe. He clasped his hands, fell to his knees, looked like he could cry. "Ah!" he said. "I am speech-less! She is more than I could have hoped for!" He trotted around the shop, fingering all the vintage thirties dresses, until he chose for the wax mannequin an emerald-green sleeveless sheath, low cut, with quivery fringes just to the knees. He placed on her head a short bobbed wig and a cloche hat, rounded, cut close to the head. He draped around her neck strings of colorful glass beads. "Aren't you the stunner,

mademoiselle!" he said when he positioned her to his satisfaction in the storefront window. Monsieur Laveau put a price
tag on the wooden mannequin. The moment he stepped away
she emitted an audible little cry.

"Ah," the Harlequin sighed with mock sympathy, "'the
course of true love never did run smooth.'"

That night the lovely wax mannequin stood in the street-
lighted storefront window in her flapper attire, in her dancing-
the-Charleston pose, her waxen face translucent on the
surface, like not-quite-frozen ice. The jester taunted one mannequin and then the other, tried earnestly to provoke a nasty
little cat fight between them for his own entertainment. But
the wooden mannequin was silent in her grief and anger, and
the wax mannequin remained cool and confident in her tri-
umph and superiority.

All night long a light burned low inside the cavity of the
wooden mannequin, like a tiny flame in a gas lamp. Then
toward morning came a sound like an amplified cough, and
the wooden mannequin blazed bright, straight, and tall, like
a torch. All the old clothes and furniture made ready fuel for
the fire, and soon the whole shop roared like the center of the
earth. The jester's harlequin jumpsuit flamed up, then poof!
Nothing was left of him but his head, which rolled across the
shelf and crashed onto the floor, shattering like a china teacup.
The wax mannequin's short bobbed wig melted; her forehead
slid down over her eyes and cheeks in thick ugly folds like the
skin of a hound. The blob that had been her elegant head
tilted slowly to one side, then slumped into her shoulder. The
fire raced like white lizards across the velvet under her feet,
up the fringes at her knees. Sirens screamed, trucks roared,
and torrents of water fell, it seemed, from the sky.

The next morning Monsieur Laveau stood in the middle of
the ruins, howling, his face covered by his oversized hands.
"Ah! I lose everything. . . . Everything!" The jester's head lay
in chips on the floor, staring up at the shopkeeper with the one
wide-open eye and raised eyebrow that remained. The Styro-
foam heads that had held the wigs lay like burnt marshmal-
lows on what remained of the mantel. The stuffed scarlet

macaw was a single black feather inside a blackened cage. With one hand Monsieur Laveau picked up off the floor all that was left of the lovely wax mannequin—a cold pale lump, a shapeless embryo lodged in a lacy puddle of cooled wax. "Oh, mademoiselle!" he cried. "*C'est tout!*" With his other hand he picked up a piece of rusted scrap metal attached by two screws to a sodden, blackened stump of wood. "And you, too, *jeune fille!*" he sobbed. "Oh, to be like you, *mes amies*! To know, to feel nothing!"

The EXCURSION

Mrs. Isabelle Oliver had been in the hospital overnight for observation, and even overnight was a week too long. She said as much to the orderly who brought in her breakfast, which Mrs. Oliver, being heavily sedated, was unable to smell, much less eat. If they didn't soon let her out of there she'd let herself out. She'd vaporize and escape through the heat vent if she had to! She had things to do! Places to go!

Oh, she knew she was talking—or was she just thinking?—outside of her head, but she couldn't help it. "I am ready to get out of here!" she announced to the maid who came in to mop the floor. The maid mopped without answering. "Past ready!" Mrs. Oliver said to the closing door after the maid rolled her mop bucket out of the room. Or she thought she said it. They had her so medicated she could hardly tell the difference between what she thought and what she said, or between yesterday, today, or 1960. "I've never been an old lie-abed like that sorry Mamie Eisenhower is," she told the nurse who came in a few minutes later to take her vital signs. "I don't care if she is the First Lady of the United States! That's no excuse for lying stretched out until noon over coffee and newspapers! I feel better than I have ever felt in my life, and I've got things to do!"

Under a fog which she supposed was induced by heavy sedation, Mrs. Oliver slept off and on most of the day, her mind a constant windy diorama. Whatever was happening now, had happened that morning or yesterday, was all muddled together: the coming and going of nurses, her daughter, Linda, kissing her on the cheek, then telling her she'd pick her up tomorrow as soon as she was discharged. Dr. Patel, that lovely woman doctor from India, standing over her, patting her hand, saying, "Mrs. Oliver, how you feel?"

"I feel fine!" she wanted to say, but she couldn't get her mouth to work, just when she needed it most. Dr. Patel had the authority to release her. She must communicate with Dr. Patel.

"We take good care of you," the doctor said.

"But I feel fine!" Mrs. Oliver tried to get the doctor to understand. She raised up in bed, or thought she did, and took hold of both of Dr. Patel's hands. "In fact I feel wonderful, doctor! So wonderful, somebody must have put ether in my IV fluids!" She had too much to do to lie here wasting away, she told the doctor. She had to clear up all the wind-blown debris of winter in her little alley garden. She had to get her garden manicured in time for all the tourists who would walk the cobblestone streets of Charleston in the spring, who would peep into her garden, snap pictures with little pocket cameras, and compare her flowers to Clara Pinckney's right next door. For an old Charlestonian like herself it was a moral imperative to have a flower garden worthy of a picture in a coffee-table book. Besides, she had so much to do to get ready for that excursion to Natchez next week with her old friend Lou Findley.

Dr. Patel patted her hand as if she understood, but then left the room without issuing orders for her release. Mrs. Oliver sighed, fell back on her pillow, and fidgeted with the bed sheets.

Minutes passed, or was it hours? Days? A nurse came into her room and took out her IV. Mrs. Oliver, certain that this was the last step before Dr. Patel came to release her, felt like she would fly up off the bed and right out the window. Still silly from sedation, she sat straight up in bed, or felt as if she did, took the nurse's face in her hands, patted her cheeks, and said, "Good girl! Good, good girl!" like the nurse was a dog who'd just rolled over at her command. "You don't know how happy you've made this old woman!" she said, smiling.

And it was true. How true. It wasn't so much because she was squeamish about having needles stuck in her veins—

goodness knows, she'd been poked and prodded so much lately that she hardly even felt it anymore. It was the anticipation of the release. She'd spent so much time in hospitals she just despised it, and she distrusted all who worked within their walls, all who scurried around like rats in and out of her room, scribbling cryptic messages about her on a chart she was never allowed to see, knowing things about her that she didn't know, fulfilling orders to take her blood or pump her with medications for reasons she was never given to understand. And the idea, the very idea, that they told her when she could leave! And it was all so militaristic! Doctor's orders. Tests. Good reports. Bad reports. Confined. Released. Discharged! Did she hear somebody say she was to be discharged? She lay there, excited, her tiny mouse hands holding the sheets up to her neck, her blue eyes opening now, twinkling like sequins in crinkled ivory velvet.

She willed herself up out of the fog. She sat up, walked over to the sink, and washed her face. She looked pale. She knew she needed to look nice and healthy when Dr. Patel came, or else the doctor might rethink letting her go. She applied a little lipstick and rouge. Now her face looked like a dried, faded tea rose, and she thought about Clara Pinckney. Clara had quite a green thumb when it came to tea roses. Her friend Lou Findley said she wouldn't believe the beautiful roses they had in the gardens in Natchez. She so looked forward to her trip in April. She ought to have traveled more. Well, it was never too late!

She packed her small overnight case, stuffing in the water pitcher, the hand towel, the little bars of Dial soap, the remote control to the TV set, and anything else that wasn't nailed down—all of which she figured she was entitled to, since either she or Medicare had paid through the nose for all of it. She had promised to call her daughter, Linda, the minute the doctor came by and discharged her, but now she decided she would do no such thing. Why bother Linda at work when she felt fine and could take the bus or a taxi home? She wanted to hang on to every thread of independence that she could. Mrs. Oliver sat on the bed, her feet dangling, her pocketbook square on her lap, her hands folded over it, ready for the doctor.

She turned and looked out the window. It was already late afternoon, and there was patchy fog over toward the harbor. It had been the kind of sweater-weather day that was rare in Charleston, except in the winter. It would have been a wonderful day for clearing up and composting, pruning the deadwood out of her shrubs, and collecting all those sad and tattered flower heads she'd been too sick to snip off back in the fall. What a mess it would be when the tulips came up, messy as an unmade bed; she couldn't bear the thought! "Mrs. Oliver, you've worn out your back," the orthopedic doctor had told her one time. "Why don't you hire somebody to do that yard work, and—"

"And do what?" she'd answered him. "Twiddle my thumbs, watch television, play bingo at the VFW?"

"Why don't you go somewhere, Mother?" Linda had said. "Especially in the summer when Charleston is hot as an African veldt, and ten times more humid. Go and spend some of that old money on yourself."

But, Mrs. Oliver thought, why go anywhere when she was already here? Most native Charlestonians know there isn't much anywhere in the world that can outshine their old city by the sea.

Oh, she had intended to go as soon as she got things squared away, but things never seemed to get squared away. She liked to think about going more than she liked to go. Unlike most people, she liked looking at travelers' brochures and itineraries before they took trips; she liked looking at their vacation pictures when they returned. It was like getting the benefit of traveling without the bother and expense. She'd finally promised to go with Lou Findley to Natchez in April.

If she got out of the hospital before April! *Now, where is that doctor?* She visualized Dr. Patel, chart in hand, making her rounds, taking her sweet time getting around to her. "How you feel?" she would say to each person in her care. Dr. Patel gave her full attention to each of her patients, which Mrs. Oliver so appreciated—as long as she was the patient.

Mrs. Oliver had a suspicion that the doctors and the hospital administration—whose purpose it was to keep people as long as possible for no reason other than to fatten their deep pockets—were in cahoots somehow. She had a vague notion that for every hour she stayed there she was running up her bill. That was not the way it was, her daughter, Linda, who was a doctor herself, had assured her, rolling her eyes, smiling indulgently at her mother. "They need beds, Mother!" she'd said. "Believe me, the last thing they want to do is detain people!" Then why, pray tell, did she always have to wait so long for a formal release, as she had in all her previous stays? Why couldn't the charge nurse release her? Good question. She pressed the buzzer to the nurses' station. No answer. Typical, typical. In this place you'd have to sound a siren to get a bedpan!

"Dr. Patel to Emergency," somebody called over the loudspeaker. "Dr. Patel to Emergency."

What a development that was! Now Dr. Patel would be detained and Mrs. Oliver would never get away. She buzzed the nurses' station again, pressing her thumb into the transmitter hard and fast, three times.

"Yes?" The nurse who answered sounded irritated.

"This is Mrs. Oliver. Yes, I said Mrs. Oliver. Now I've waited and waited and buzzed and buzzed and tried to be patient. I fully expected to be discharged today. I've been waiting here, packed and ready to go for the better part of an hour. I will not—I repeat—I will not spend another night here!"

"Mrs. Oliver? Mrs. Oliver?"

She didn't answer. She'd already spoken her piece. She felt a satisfaction when the nurses got a dose of their own medicine—let them be on the receiving end. Let them get a foretaste of what it's like to be old and ignored. She'd take matters into her own hands, as she ought to have done from the get-go. What could they do if they caught her? Put her on trial for going AWOL? She took her night bag and her pocketbook and slipped out of the room, embarking, she felt, on an escape where she was a prisoner, and every face was that of a guard or the warden.

She saw an orderly rolling a dinner cart down the hall, but thankfully he had his head down getting a covered plate from the second tier and didn't see her. She tiptoed in the opposite direction to the service elevator at the end of the hall, barely escaping the notice of the two nurses who were, as an apparent response to her call, hurrying to her room with startled looks on their faces. She stepped into the elevator, which was occupied by some drab young girl in a lab coat who paid her no notice, and went down to the lobby. She tiptoed across the lobby, skittish as a roach in sudden light. She had just reached the hospital exit when a white-haired man, volunteering at the help desk, looked up.

"Good evening," he said. He eyed the plastic identity bracelet that in her haste to escape she had not taken off, took her hand, read the bracelet, and said, "Mrs. Oliver?"

She nodded and headed like a missile toward the door, only to have the man grab her arm. "May I help you?" he asked. "May I direct you somewhere?"

"No, thank you. I'm quite sure where I'm headed."

"Are you, Mrs. Oliver? Are you quite sure?" He followed her to the door.

The fog, she could see now, had moved in from the harbor. "Why, of course I'm sure!" she snapped. Few people could be as irritating as an overly earnest volunteer.

"If I may ask, have you been properly released? Did your doctor discharge you?"

"Now, why would you think otherwise?"

"Well, it is a hospital regulation that all discharged patients are wheeled to the exit in a wheelchair, whereas you, Mrs. Oliver, arrived at the lobby on foot and, I might add, all in a dither."

Regulations again! Now that she was identified as an escapee, time was of the essence. Thankfully, she was still spry and fleet of foot. She pushed her way past the volunteer and a man on crutches to get out the door.

But the volunteer was fast behind her, barreling after her, bandy-legged, across the pavement, waving her down. "Mrs. Oliver! Please!"

She slipped away into the fog. Not far from the entrance, the hospital parking shuttle pulled up and its double doors swung open. "Do you go past the city bus stop?" she asked. The driver nodded without speaking or looking her way. He closed the doors and pulled away before she had properly situated herself in her seat, and she nearly lost her footing. "Oh!" she said. He turned the steering wheel with his right hand only. His left arm hung out the open window.

"Would you mind closing that window?" she asked, as politely as she could. "I just got out of the hospital, and the foggy, fumy air is not good for my respiratory function." He didn't close it and he didn't answer. "I'll give you the benefit of the doubt," she said. "Perhaps you're hard of hearing?" She spoke louder, so loud her voice cracked: "I said, 'do you mind shutting that window!'" He did nothing, said nothing. "Well! Of all the inconsiderate. . . !" It was enough to make a preacher cuss!

She searched for his face in the rearview mirror, but the mirror was turned in such a way that nothing showed in it but his knees. "I take it you don't have an old mother like me. If you do, I pity her. You must be a very bad son!" With trembling fingers she rummaged through her pocketbook until she found the clear plastic hair bonnet, folded up like an accordion, that she always kept with her in case of foul weather. She unfolded it and wrapped it around her head as a shield against the damp air inside the bus and so she'd be all ready when she stepped off the shuttle at the bus stop. "Luckily, we will soon part company!" she barked, fumbling to tie the strings at her neck. "And it will not be a moment too soon!"

Mrs. Oliver sat forward in the seat, clutching her pocketbook to her stomach, and tried to soothe her jumpy nerves by looking through the thin fog at the earliest spring blooms: the deep yellow of forsythia, the white Yoshino cherry and Bradford pear trees that adorned the parking lots and medical office parks. They passed the parking lots of Radiology, Emergency, and Admitting, where no one waited to be picked up, so the driver did not stop. Then they passed right by the always-lighted "Rx" sign at the pharmacy, where she intended to get on the city bus. "Excuse me! You've gone right past my stop!" But he kept right on going, with no explanation whatsoever. "If you'll stop and let me off here, please!" He drove on. What to do? Should she put down the window and yell for help? Why, of course not! What would the Pinckneys, the Middletons, or the Ravenels say if they heard tell of Isabelle Oliver riding along in a bus with her head hanging out the window like a dog?

The bus went on, making a wider circle around the hospital complex, circling and circling, until she thought they must have come near the harbor, so thick was the fog now. It was like a gray fleece blanket wrapped around the bus. She felt uneasy, like the bus had become airborne, like she was in a blimp sailing through a cloud. She had no idea the hospital shuttle went out that far, and she could not imagine why it would.

She leaned forward in her seat and shook her finger at the driver. "I demand to know where you are taking me!" she shouted. The driver said nothing, and Mrs. Oliver was overcome by a sudden chill. She had often wondered about people who drove the same circuitous routes hour after hour, day after day. So much monotony might breed madness. He might hit her over the head and dump her somewhere far from town where she would disintegrate into the elements like a dead seagull, without a proper burial or even a notice in the newspaper. Should she pummel him over the head with her pocketbook? No, she didn't have the strength for that. She rummaged through her purse. "Look here," she said, her voice high pitched, her fingers and every nerve in her body quivering. "I've got these bills from when I got my Social Security check cashed right before I went into the hospital. I need to hold back twenty or thirty dollars for my prescriptions, but you can have the rest of it if you'll just stop and let me out."

The bus continued on for a while, then stopped with a sudden lurch, throwing Mrs. Oliver forward. Clutching her pocketbook under one arm, holding her overnight bag in the other, she made her way on unsure feet, stumbling, to the front. The driver stared straight ahead—insolent!—and shook his head at the money Mrs. Oliver offered. *Well*, she thought, *they say there's a little bit of good even in the worst of us.* The door swung open, and Mrs. Oliver scrambled out.

When the bus pulled away she realized she was all alone in fog thick as she-crab soup, in a place without a single landmark she could see. And with evening coming on! She might be standing in the middle of the street, for all she knew, but a street without any traffic she could see or hear. Once the last sounds of the shuttle bus died away, she could hear water slapping hard against a shoreline.

So she was near the harbor! Or near some body of water, anyway. Her suitcase in one hand, her pocketbook in the other, Mrs. Oliver walked blindly a few feet in what she thought might be the direction of the water, and then a few more feet forward, until finally she saw a small dome outlined by very dim lights.

Straining her eyes through the fog, she could see that it was a gazebo. She was able to make out, as she walked a little closer, that there was a boat dock beyond the gazebo, and past that, dark, liverish, choppy water. Where in the world was she? It certainly wasn't City Pier, or any dock she recognized, but there was nothing so unusual about that. There were many public docks she knew nothing about, and there must be hundreds of private docks in and around any port city. She could be anywhere!

The fog thinned for a moment, like a curtain held back from a window, and she could see people standing under the domed roof, huddled against the dampness. They were men and women, many at or around her age, she guessed, though one younger woman caught her eye. She had dark hair long as a stallion's tail. She stood apart from the others, looking seaward, her hands tight on the railing, her chin uplifted, her upper body inclined forward, like a figurehead on the prow of a ship. And there was one child, a boy, playing at the edge of the water. But most were white haired like herself, well-dressed tourists, as best she could tell.

Oh, she was so thankful to see somebody, anybody, now that it was getting so near dark. She was as excited as if she'd just run across old friends. She noticed a thickening in the gray distance, a boat or a ferry with lights that shone dim through the foggy, deepening night, moving slowly toward the dock. A harbor tour, of course! To Fort Sumter? No, it was much too late in the day for that. She'd heard about moonlight excursions into the harbor and always meant to go on one. Were they waiting for the tour boat? Little chance for moonlight this evening, not in this thick fog. Well, anyway, maybe one of those people would know where the nearest bus stop was—tourists were better at that than natives. Locals tended not to know much about city services except for the ones they used themselves every day. She started across the boardwalk to the steps leading up to the gazebo.

She heard little snatches of conversation. Maybe the heavy fog would lift during the passage, someone said. Wouldn't that be lovely? A full moon over the harbor! Could be a rough ride over the choppy water, said one anxious voice. It might be, another voice said, that the attractions on the other side will more than make up for a less-than-perfect journey. Mrs. Oliver started up the steps thinking she might just stay and chat with them until their ferry arrived. They certainly seemed like pleasant enough people, and she was genuinely curious to find out just where it was they were all waiting to go.

Lost SOUL

At nine o'clock it finally cleared. The full moon hung in the upper-left pane of the window, and the broad dune field between the houses and the surf glowed pale oyster. Leigh knew the walk over to Bird Island would be well-lighted, though it might be all the more eerie because of it. She didn't care. She was dying to get out of the house where she'd been stuck with Kayla, her unappreciative stepdaughter, for two days of what was supposed to be a long weekend.

For two weary, dreary days she had looked out the same bay window from where she had watched the continuous sea changes over many summers in her youth. Two days of pale-pewter sky and olive-green ocean. A cold, steady rain had speckled the dunes. But now it was clear, and the moon was full. She slipped on a jacket. "I thought I'd take a walk over Bird Island way," she said to Kayla. "Interested?"

The light from the TV screen flashed like a strobe across Kayla's narrow face. She sat unmoved and unspeaking, like a statue in a park during a fireworks display.

"Going to bed early," Kayla finally said in a small, disembodied voice.

Sometimes Leigh felt like grabbing Kayla by her shoulders and shaking her. How she could feel such hostility—yes, hostility—for this child, who was bone of the bone of the man she'd loved most in all the world?

"Suit yourself, then," Leigh said, her voice tight. "I'll see you in the morning." She was halfway out the door when she stopped and added, "It's time for us to talk, Kayla. Past time. And we will talk. In the car on the way home tomorrow." Silence. Leigh let the door slam shut and started across the boardwalk over the dunes.

For the past two days Kayla had barely said a word. She had lain splayed out on the couch under the dim light of the ship-in-a-bottle lamp, the same lamp that had been gathering dust in that spot since the years Leigh and her parents had stayed in that same cottage. Kayla had watched TV, flipped through *Vogue* magazine, twirled a lock of her hair around her forefinger. She'd taken a break from that only to scrape loose the red polish from the nail on her big toe. A pile of magazines had avalanched on the floor beside the sofa. A Coke can had made Olympic rings on the coffee table. Leigh did not understand; when she was that age nobody had needed to tell her not to live like a pig.

But, to be fair, Leigh thought while ambling down the boardwalk, pulling up the hood of her coat against the chill, *Kayla, lovesick over some boy, hadn't wanted to come*. The little beach trip was a clumsy scheme Leigh had come up with to heal the dis-ease between them, to give them the chance to become, if never mother and daughter, at least something akin to friends.

But Kayla had never been to any beach but Myrtle, and she couldn't understand why anybody would go to any beach in October. Leigh tried to get her to see the appeal of a beach like Sunset, where high dunes banked weathered cottages that had been built far back from the shoreline. Kayla complained it took too long to get from the doorstep to the beach. Leigh pointed out that some refuge for wildlife remained here, and the ocean was still center stage. Kayla said it was "the boringest place on Earth."

Here in the fall, the sea oats had turned golden. The sea lavender had turned its namesake color, and the skies were noisy with migrating birds. Kayla was blind to it. Leigh had hoped for an hour or two of clear weather so she could get Kayla to walk with her over to Bird Island. It was a ritual of Leigh's girlhood, that walk, but Kayla couldn't have been less interested.

They were not friends right now, Leigh and Kayla. They hadn't been since Gary's single-engine Cessna had gone down over Deep Gap just under a year ago, making Leigh a widow and Kayla fatherless, leaving them alone to battle it out or to bond. It had been mostly battle.

"Try to remember when you were that age," a friend of Leigh's, a mother of three teenagers, advised her when Kayla had been caught buying a drink underage.

"I do remember," she said. "I remember that at that age I went out of my way to avoid trouble."

"You need to do more than make rules," the friend said, gently, when Kayla came in past curfew and Leigh was beside herself about it. "Kids these days have minds of their own. They have to know why."

"When I was that age," Leigh told her, "I didn't need any explanations."

And so it had gone. Kayla's crack-addict mother was hardly fit to raise her. So now Leigh, an architect who had been careful not to draft children into the blueprint of her life, had a fourteen-year-old daughter to raise. Four years until Kayla was eighteen. Four years until freedom.

Leigh stopped midway on the walk from the doorstep to the beach and looked back. She saw Kayla standing in the window, looking out to sea, her face mournful like a widow watching for her sea-captain husband who was never to return. Kayla looked so small in the window, her long hair hanging over that little sad-sack face.

Kayla, as if she could sense Leigh's judgment, turned and walked away, her hair swinging around like the mane of a haughty show horse. Leigh shook her head. At that age she had been aware of boys, certainly, but she hadn't obsessed over them.

Or had she? As Leigh stepped out onto the sand and took up the slow, meditative stride of the seasoned beach walker, she thought of Mark Wyatt. She couldn't walk over to Bird Island without thinking about Mark Wyatt, the gorgeous, the glorious, the one who was as unreachable as the moon that now hung between the fishing pier and the arc of the sky. She took in a deep breath of healing, briny air, took in the broad sweeping emptiness, the rise and the fall of the surf. Moonlight rocked on the waves in wedges of spun silver. The sea oats and the shore shrubs cast deep shadows on the dunes, but it was remarkably bright.

It was darker to the west, toward Bird Island, which was not actually an island anymore. Currents had so reconfigured the landscape that what was once Mad Inlet was now a long, windswept, sandy isthmus stretching over to the maritime jungle everybody still called Bird Island. She could see the island in the distance. In the moonlight the trees near its shore looked like a photographic negative.

"Were you really such a saint back in your youth?" the friend who counseled her about Kayla had wanted to know. Well, no. The truth was, back then she'd been accused more than once of being a conniving little witch. Enterprising, she preferred to think of it now. Yes. She'd been enterprising in trying to work her way into Mark Wyatt's field of vision. It hadn't worked, though. No, she had hardly been a saint that long-ago summer, and now, for some reason, that nagged at her like a sandspur lodged in the heel.

To her left the tide eased forward. This was the spot where the family of Kennedy-esque Wyatts had played. Here Mark had swam, surfed. Even now she felt like she was walking hallowed ground. How silly to think that. How silly she had been back then!

Mark Wyatt had been tall and tawny, with blond hair bleached white by the sun and a face that looked like it had been carved by a sculptor. It was the kind of face that would have been too pretty if it hadn't been for the strong jaw, wide mouth, big teeth. He was everything that mattered in those days. He had been near the top of his class at their high school, had been a track star. Every woman had a Mark Wyatt in her memory, a never-forgotten first love that in her mind had been elevated to legend.

The Mark Wyatts of the world were always unattainable. They broke hearts effortlessly, just by maintaining their cool distance. She'd watched his every move through junior high and high school, had written his name in textbooks, had consulted the Ouija board about him during silly girls' games at pajama parties. She had even audited an algebra class she'd already taken in hopes of getting his attention. But she was not the kind of girl who would have attracted the notice of a star like Mark—he could have had his pick from the cheerleading squad or the homecoming court. He'd spoken to her in the doorway of the gym once, and she'd lived off the glory of it for the rest of the year.

She wondered whatever became of him. She was sure he had become something big and wonderful, had married a perfect and perfectly beautiful woman, no doubt, and had wonderful, accomplished children. She had spoken to him, briefly, at their ten-year high school reunion. He had changed and she'd been, inevitably, a little disappointed. She had seen him, only in passing, two or three times since. That was not unusual. She could count on one hand the classmates she'd kept up with. But the young Mark of her girlhood summer, Mark the beach boy, lived on in memory.

After a little while, she walked past Sunset Beach's final string of houses, all set far behind the dunes, all closed up for the season. Among them was the house where the Wyatts had stayed that summer. It was the last house before Mad Inlet, or where Mad Inlet had once been. Back then everybody called it the "End House." The upstairs windows of the house peeped like a crab above the dunes.

That summer had been her summer of destiny. She could laugh about it now, but back then that was how she had thought about the summer the Wyatts had stayed in the End House. It was the summer before Mark, who graduated from West two years before her, would go off to Duke. Leigh was not yet sixteen.

She was washing the sand off her feet in the outdoor shower stall when Mama came back from gathering up sand dollars. Guess who she'd run into? Mama said. Loreen Wyatt! Everybody back home in Charlotte knew who the Wyatts were. They were well-off and well-thought-of people who were connected to anything and everything progressive or charitable. They were known for spearheading prison min-

istries and taking in foster children and so-called marginal-
ized youth. Leigh's mother, simple-minded Suzy Sunshine
that she was, always thought the best of people, so she
believed the Wyatts were just wonderful. But Daddy wasn't
all that impressed with the Wyatts' do-goodism after he heard
they boarded so many youth offenders. He couldn't understand why a man, in the interest of compassion for others,
would take in somebody who could cause harm to his family. Leigh's mother said she was sure they didn't take in just
anybody. The Wyatts were good people, smart people. They
wouldn't take in somebody they had reason to be afraid of.

"Loreen says they'll be here for two whole weeks," Mama
told Leigh. "And they're staying right there at the End
House."

"The whole family?" Leigh held her breath for the answer.

Mama nodded. "All the Wyatts, plus one. Them and a trou-
bled boy they've taken in for a while." Leigh couldn't believe
it. The End House! Just a short stroll away. Leigh held her
head under the shower spray to hide the beatific glow on her
face. She felt like the universe had aligned everything in her
favor.

From the bay window of the beach cottage, with one of
many pairs of high-powered binoculars that Mama, a dedicated bird watcher, always had lying around, Leigh studied
the habits of the Wyatts just as Mama watched the gulls, terns,
and egrets. Just as Daddy, surf fishing, watched the skies for
flocks of seagulls to tell where schools of bluefish were running, Leigh watched Mr. and Mrs. Wyatt, Mark's younger
brother, and his two sisters—all identifiable as Wyatts by their
taut, tan, athletic good looks—sun, swim, play volleyball,
touch football.

The "plus one" Mama had mentioned was a thin, long-
armed, dark-haired boy who orbited at a distance around the
bright constellation of Wyatts—cold, dark, and distant, like
the planet Pluto. He joined in their games only when Mark
waved him into them. He swam a lot, this boy, whose name,
Leigh would learn, was Ben. She would have the binoculars
trained on the spit of sand that was the Wyatt playground,

waiting for any one of the stars to appear on their stage, when, at the outer edge of the binocular lenses, she would see Ben, his head coursing through the waves like the head of a shark, his dark, wiry arms like tentacles of a squid as he fought the waves. Ben especially liked to swim in the rough water before or after a storm. Leigh would see him sulking on the porch steps or walking up and down the beach, scanning the sand with a metal detector. Years later she would realize that Ben had been encased in a dusky nimbus, within which he was safe, and others safe from him.

But she soon stopped seeing Ben or Mark's parents or siblings, just as her mama ceased to see ordinary seagulls for fear she'd miss the brief appearance of a black-bellied plover. Leigh let Ben and the Wyatts fade into the background while she saw only Mark. Mark as he sat on the front porch polishing his surfboard, Mark as he rode the silky waves of early morning, the rough and rugged waves of afternoon.

"What's that you're looking at so hard?" Mama asked her that first morning after she'd learned the Wyatts were there.

"A black-bellied plover," Leigh said, right off the top of her head.

Mama, excited, took the binoculars and looked to see for herself. "Where?" she asked, all innocence. "Where?"

The next day Leigh spread out her blanket not far from the End House. She made a big production of slicking herself from forehead to toe tips with coconut oil. She stood up and smoothed out her beach towel when it wasn't bunched up. She would get up every now and then, swinging her long hair over her shoulders, and peer through the binoculars to the horizon, as if watching for ships or schools of dolphins. But Mark Wyatt, already surrounded by girls who seemed to have washed up like sirens in the tide overnight, never looked her way.

Even now, all these years later, she blushed at how she'd acted like a bird doing a mating dance. And for what? Heartache.

Then, the third day after the Wyatts arrived, she'd been almost put to sleep by the drone of the surf. Her eyes were closed, her face was hidden from the sun under a paperback novel she hadn't been able to get into. She felt the sand stir beside her. She looked over and started. A boy stood not three feet from her. It was Ben. He was bent over poking his finger into a clear blob, veined and pinkish. It looked like a harvested brain.

She shot up and pulled her bathing suit straps up over her shoulders.

"Sorry," he said, his voice low, tight. "Didn't mean to scare you." Ben was somewhere around her age, she guessed. Skinny, white tee shirt, cut-off jeans, dark, stick-straight, thistly hair. Small dark eyes that met hers, put up a wall, then darted away. She had known his type in school. The kind who is the prize victim of many a school bully and is hardened by it. The kind who had all but closed himself off but still craved contact with people, and could be childish and clumsy about getting it.

"That's okay," she said. She sat up, turned away from him, and pretended to be engrossed in the novel, hoping he would leave. He didn't. He stayed and poked again at the jellyfish. "That jellyfish will sting you," she warned.

"It's not a jellyfish," he said. "It's sea pork."

"Oh." She turned the page of the novel and pretended to read.

He turned over the blob and pointed to the little white specks on it. "Those are little mouths that pump water and decayed plants into the body. That's how they eat."

"Interesting," she said, and poked her nose deeper into the book.

"Yo! Ben!" somebody called. "Mom said come on! Lunchtime!" They both looked up toward the End House. It was Mark, rubbing a beach towel across his back, calling to Ben from the front porch. Leigh's heart lurched at the sight of him. Mark's eyes lit on her face for half a second, like a fly. He didn't seem to recognize her, or worse, didn't care to acknowledge her. Two feet away a sand crab scuttled into a hole. She wished she could do the same. Ben threw up his hand to Mark, then started up the beach.

"Wait, Ben," Leigh said. She sat up, swung her hair over

her shoulders, wrapped her arms around her knees. Ben, she suddenly realized, might be her one last thin thread of connection with Mark Wyatt. "So, you're one of the Wyatts?" she asked, though she knew better.

Ben looked at her, eyes blank. He took a while to answer. "I'm not anybody," he said finally. His tone was not childish, not self-pitying, not ironic. It came across as plain fact, plainly stated, and for that reason it struck a chill in her. With both hands he tenderly picked up the sea pork and carried it past the surf into waist-high water. He struggled past a cross current, cradled the sea pork within the waves, and watched it ride out to sea. As if to avoid having to face Leigh again, he didn't return to the stretch of beach where she was. He swam with the current in the direction of the End House, passed it, then tumbled in with the tide. Wet and dark as an otter, he strode up the beach to the End House. The frayed thread, Leigh felt sure, had already broken.

She felt even worse when, that afternoon, Mama told her that Loreen Wyatt had asked them all up there for a fish fry. She had made up some excuse why they couldn't go. "Mama!" Leigh cried, then she ran over and threw herself on the sofa and buried her head in her arms.

"Well, what did you want me to say?" Mama asked, bewildered. "You know your daddy can't stand socializing in the first place. And he has never cared for 'those do-gooder Wyatts!'"

Leigh thought she would die. "Oh, Mama! How could you refuse an invitation from the Wyatts?"

"Well that doesn't mean you can't go," her mama said. "I'm sure they'd be glad to have you. You want me to call Loreen and—"

"No!"

"Well, just show up at the door. I'm sure they won't turn you away."

"Oh!" Leigh covered her head with a pillow and sobbed. No, she didn't want to go with Mama into Shallotte to shop. She didn't want to go back on the beach. She didn't want to live to get her driver's license or go to college. She wanted to die.

But she didn't die. Instead she spent the latter part of the afternoon sadly watching the happy Wyatt habitat from her station at the bay window or from the front deck. She looked past Daddy surf fishing for blues—pants legs rolled up, tanned hairy legs planted firmly in the swash—to watch Mark and family, all gleaming, muscular energy, playing a rousing game of volleyball. She watched Mark emerge from a swim with two girls in loud-colored bikinis, girls colorful and sparkling as tropical fish. With the binoculars she could see the sand glistening off the tawny hairs of Mark's legs and the white skin just above the band of his swim trunks.

Ben, scanning the sand with a metal detector, walked up from the east end of the beach and scurried toward the house like a raccoon, staying well clear of the playing Wyatts. They all stopped to call him into the game. Ben shook his head and walked toward the porch. Mark excused himself from the company and followed him. They sat side by side on the porch, Ben, his head hung low, Mark, his face turned to Ben. Mark's face looked grave and seeking, like a counselor's. Leigh was to see similar scenes many times. Later, as the sun went down, a crowd gathered at the Wyatt house. Music blasted. Lights burned from every window. Leigh lay on the couch feeling like the whole world was on top of a pole and she was at the bottom of it.

Later that night a storm came up. The next morning, though the sea was again calm, the beach looked all different. Daddy left to go deep-sea fishing, and Mama had gone to the hospital in Southport to see a friend.

Through the binoculars Leigh saw Ben pacing in the sand around some dark, long-shaped something that had washed up overnight. She wasn't interested in Ben or what he had found, but she knew Mark, who liked to surf in early morning, would come soon.

When she got closer, she saw that the washed-up something was nothing more than an old timber, gray and pitted with wear. Mark, his surfboard under his arm, came to see it, too. Leigh couldn't have been less curious about it. "What is that?" she asked Ben, just as Mark came along.

Mark nodded to Leigh, then spoke. "Yeah, what'd you find there, Ben?"

"It's a hull plank from an old ship," Ben said.

"Might be an old pirate ship, huh?" Mark asked.

"A pirate ship?" Leigh echoed, sounding fascinated. "No kidding?"

"An old pirate ship from seventeen hundred and something," Ben said.

"Geez, buddy," Mark said. "I don't know how you know all you do." Mark cast Leigh a searching look. "Don't you go to West?" She nodded. "I thought you looked kind of familiar. Well, good to see you." There might have been some possibility of a conversation, but one of yesterday's girls walked in their direction, stopped, hands on hips, cocked her head, and waited. Mark gave Ben a quick slap on the back and was off again.

Leigh, heartsick, spent that afternoon and the next two days walking the beach with Ben while he combed the sand with a metal detector. If Daddy had been around more he would have had something to say about that, but he had gone with some fishing cronies up to Hatteras and was to be gone for many days. Mama planned several all-day excursions to barrier islands to photograph shorebirds.

On the beach Ben found what he said was a hook from a Confederate soldier's knapsack. "Isn't that something?" Leigh said, but she was watching the surf, choppy that day, where Mark had taken a tumble. She held her breath until his blond head bobbed up between the waves like a buoy.

Now, many years later, a buoy caught Leigh's attention again. White in the moonlight, it bobbed in the choppy water around the shoals where Mad Inlet had once made a broad cut into the shoreline. A sign told her she was leaving Sunset Beach, entering what had once been Bird Island. The beach was very flat. The swash kept it spare, with no dunes and no vegetation to hold back wind or water. The wind swept across it, batting at her sleeves and the hood of her jacket. In a little while, when the tide came in, it would sweep in swiftly, unhindered. She had never lost her appreciation for the awe-some power of the ocean. She stepped up her pace to a quick stride, slowing only to pick up a whelk shell that shone like a giant pearl in the sand near the surf. It was perfect as a cut gem and fit neatly in the palm of her hand.

With some years between then and now Leigh could see the selfishness of what she had done.

"What have you got there, Ben?" she said, one early morning, when from the bay window she'd seen him walking on the beach. Knowing Mark would soon be around, she'd hurried out to walk with him. He jumped a little, startled at her approach. He smiled when he saw her, but didn't speak. There was something unhinged about him that morning. She really saw then, for the first time, that he suffered from some deep and private pain.

Hadn't she had the slightest twinge of empathy? Not that she could recall.

"Oh, a conch shell," she said, when he held out what he had found. It was almost black, with a myriad of tiny holes in it. She'd picked up and thrown back several like it over the years. "I don't believe I've ever seen a conch like that before," she said.

"It's a whelk shell," he said. "You hardly ever find real conchs except in the Caribbean. It's a whelk shell." He stooped down and sloshed it in the clear water of the tidal pool, poked his finger as far as he could into the inner spiral of it to make sure, he told her, that nothing was alive in there.

There was a tight, unreachable place inside Ben, she remembered thinking that day. Nobody could get to it, just as a finger cannot reach around to the place in a shell where the spiral ends.

Leigh asked Ben how long he had been with the Wyatts, while they walked up the beach, down the beach, over to Bird Island and back. He and Mark didn't seem to share many interests. Were he and Mark good friends? To Leigh's disappointment, he didn't have much to say about Mark.

Like many a lone wolf, once Ben felt the least bit easy talking about himself, he was hard to stop. He was from Crusoe

Island, he said, in the Green Swamp, thirty, forty miles inland. He bet she'd never heard of it. No, she said, she'd never heard of Crusoe Island. Green Swamp she did know about, though. They passed through it on the way to the beach. It was the last long stretch of road, an endless stretch of nothing, not a place you wanted to have car trouble. His ancestors had been Portuguese pirates, he said. Three hundred years ago they'd moved inland to escape the law.

Now, more than twenty years later, Leigh would want to hear all about Ben's history, but back then she had one pressing interest, and that was Mark.

"Hiya, Leigh," Mark would say, when he met them on the beach or on the front porch. Mark's eyes lingered on her face a few seconds longer than they used to, as if he was right before telling or asking her something. "What you got there, Ben?" he'd say. He'd look over the Civil War coin, or the toe tap from a Confederate soldier's shoe. Ben was always finding those things on the beach. "You're sure some detective, Ben."

Into the second week of the Wyatts' stay, through her friendship with Ben, Leigh had finally managed to worm her way into the Wyatt's circle, into their volleyball matches and Frisbee throws, into lunch with the family.

And, she was sickened to see, into Ben's heart.

One day after lunch, Leigh and Ben were in the swing on the porch of the End House. The Wyatt sisters were lying in the sun. The girls' parents had gone walking up the beach, and Mark had gone to get something done to the car. Ben held a section of a horse's jaw with teeth still on it. It was from a pirate's mount, he said. The wood-handled knife encrusted with coral had belonged to a pirate as well. She shuddered at the horse jaw. She didn't like the knife either, or Ben's fascination with it, even though the only thing sharp about it was the jagged coral attached to it like cement.

"I bet you've never known anybody who was a descendant of pirates," he said. He'd said that more than once. No, she hadn't, she said. "There's a saying in my family: Bad blood runs downhill. If you knew everything about me, you might not feel the way you do."

Leigh felt panic. What did he mean by that? She didn't feel anything for him, not even pity. She had never known anyone for whom she'd had less feeling.

Looking back, she understood that Ben, like many a drowning man, had gotten hold of a rope and was grabbing on too hard, working his way up it too fast.

She got up to leave, made some excuse. He grabbed her arm and held her back. It was still low tide. Wouldn't she walk over to Bird Island with him? There was good fishing in the creek. He'd like her company. She half heard him, nodded. Mark had driven up. She heard Mark crooning with the radio, heard the car door slam.

"You will?"

"Will what?"

"Walk over to Bird Island since it's low tide?"

"Not today, Ben. It won't be long before the tide comes back in. By the time we get over there we'll have to turn right around and come back."

"I'd really like it if you would."

"Oh alright, alright," she said, never intending to go at all. Ben went out back to the tank where he kept bait. She got up to run home, but just then Mark stopped at the refrigerator, then stepped out onto the porch.

"Hiya, Leigh," he said. "Where you going?"

She shrugged, then sat back down in the swing. Mark took Ben's place beside her. He smelled like salt spray and Coppertone. He took a swig from a bottle of Dr. Pepper and looked into the house to make sure Ben was out of earshot. "Look, Leigh. I've been dying for a chance to talk to you." She poked her hair behind her ears, looked down at her toes. She felt dizzy.

"You know, I've been watching you the past few days," he said.

"You have?" Her heart swelled.

"Tried not to be obvious about it." *Oh, don't worry, you haven't been*, she thought, but didn't say. "I've been watching you with Ben. I can see Ben's got a little thing for you." Her heart fell. He glanced in the doorway again. He bent over, clasped his hands between his knees. "Listen, I think it's real sweet of you to be so nice to him, but be careful."

"What do you mean?"

"Well, Ben's the kind of guy you don't want to get the wrong idea. He's had a hard time. Some hard, hard knocks. He was beat up as a kid, passed from pillar to post."

"You mean I ought to be afraid of Ben?"

He shook his head, seemed to think before answering. "I don't think that. I don't think Pop would have taken him in if he thought that. I don't think Ben has any kind of criminal record or anything. I'd just hate to see Ben hurt, is all. Just don't give him any reason to feel too attached, you know." She nodded. "But don't let him off too quick or too hard, either. That might be the hard part."

She nodded. He patted her on the knee, took up his surfboard, and started for the beach.

Ben came out with a pail of live shrimp and a fishing rod. "You ready to go?"

"Ben, I—" She watched Mark easing out into the waves.

"You said you would."

So she walked with Ben over to Bird Island. They waded over in knee-deep water, but when the tide came in they would have to swim back, and Leigh was a poor swimmer. She followed Ben across the high dunes. The dunes were higher on Bird Island than on Sunset Beach. She was hot, weary, and felt like she was climbing over a mountain range. She followed him deeper into a thicket of yaupon to a dark, winding tidal creek where he said the fishing was good. She looked back. "The tide's already starting to come in," she said. "I'm not a good swimmer."

"So, what's the worst that could happen?"

"We'd be stuck here overnight."

He shrugged. "That wouldn't be so bad, would it?"

The maritime woods were dark, tropical. There was no sound but the singing of insects, and surf, which seemed a long way off. She felt lonely for the sight of Sunset Beach across Mad Inlet. She thought of the tide rushing in as she sat there, deep water covering the shoals. She felt like she was stranded on an island far out to sea. But most of all, she was mad at Ben for being such a waste of her time, for turning out to be the wrong means to her end.

"Why do you look so sad?" Ben asked her. He was baiting the hook. She looked at the live shrimp struggling against it, then laid her head over her knees and cried. He put his hand on her head. "It takes live shrimp to lure trout in these creeks," he said. "But I don't have to do it, if it bothers you. I don't have to fish at all."

No, no. That wasn't it at all.

He took the shrimp off the hook and dropped it in the bucket. Oh, he had read her so wrong. She looked at him, thinking how she might explain. He touched his fingers to her cheeks, like it was the first time he'd ever seen tears.

She took his hand and pulled it away. "Look, Ben, I think you've got the wrong idea." She spoke hard, harder than she meant to.

"About what?"

"About me . . . and . . . you."

His eyes went black as shark teeth. "You think because I don't say much I don't see what goes on. You think I don't know you used me like bait."

He stood up and kicked the live shrimp, pail and all, into the creek. She ran. He dogged her the long way down the banks of the creek and across the dunes. She knew he could have caught up with her at any time, but he stalked her slowly, steadily, as if he preferred to let her do the running through the deep hot sand, knowing she would wear herself out quickly, and then. . . .

At Mad Inlet the tide was rushing in. He followed her part of the way in, sloshing through the shin-deep water in slow motion. But then he stopped and watched her struggle through the middle, where the water went suddenly from knee-deep to waist-deep. From the other side, she looked back and saw him standing unmoved and unmoving, dark and still in the water as a pier piling.

That night a fire burned several acres of forest on Bird Island. The Wyatts and all the people staying in houses on the west end of the beach came out to watch. It was an awful spectacle, that conflagration across Mad Inlet.

She could see it now, could smell the smoke, hear the roar of the Coast Guard firefighting boats.

Leigh had to answer questions from the sheriff, and she felt like an accomplice to a crime. Daddy came back from deep-sea fishing and had words with Mr. Wyatt. Leigh and her parents packed up and left that same day.

Now, twenty-some years later, Leigh arrived again at what had once been the shore of Bird Island. The sand climbed into high dunes and was absorbed by the dark woods. Bright eyes stared back at her from a thicket. Deer, raccoon, or owl?

She had done it. She had made the ritual walk. And it had been pleasant, except for the one unpleasant memory. The wind was wilder over here. The tide was coming in. She turned and started back the way she had come.

Their house, the house where she and Kayla were staying, was hidden behind a larger house this side of it. It seemed farther going back than it had coming. She was not ready to go back just yet. The End House was close by. From behind the dunes its porch windows gave back the moonlight. She crossed the long boardwalk to the End House, passing through a tunnel of tall-growing yaupon, myrtle, and yucca. She climbed the steps to the porch and sat on the swing. There, behind the dunes, the surf sound died down to a hush like the sound in a seashell held to the ear. The scene toward the ocean looked like an old picture postcard of a moonlit beach, the colors strange, unreal. The house, like the others near it, was closed up for winter. The rusty chains creaked as she slowly swung back and forth, back and forth. In the window her shadow swung like the shadow of a clock pendulum. She wondered if the Wyatts had ever come back here.

She had run into Mark at a business affair in Charlotte. He was slightly heavier, his hairline had started to recede, and he had seemed ordinary. Over cocktails she asked about his family, and, more to seem polite than because she really wondered, she had asked him about Ben. He had lived the kind of life his early years had predicted, Mark said. He had done some time in prison. He had lived for a while in a shack a couple of miles inland, had died years ago of a self-inflicted gunshot wound. His body was found adrift in a small fishing boat in a cove of the dark and winding Lockwood Folly River. That river, she knew, emptied just east of here.

Odd that now, all these years later, she felt the first real surge of pity for lost souls like Ben, the misused and abused. The tide was rolling in. The full-moon tide sounded like thunder. Two shadows swung side by side in the window next to her, or so it seemed. She was tired now, and seeing double. She stepped out. The swing eased to a stop. It started up again on its own, slowly, back and forth, back and forth. It was the wind, only the wind. The swing stopped. One end twisted slightly as if somebody had stepped out of it. Again only the wind. The wind could do strange things.

She walked—quickly, yes—but she refused to run. A steady walk down the porch steps across the long, long, boardwalk, through the dark tunnel of dune shrubs. Something tugged at her sleeve. The spikes of the yucca shrubs, she was sure. Faster down the steps into the sand, down the beach. The sand above the waterline made for hard walking, so she veered down to the hard-packed wet sand. The surf rolled and thundered. Beyond the breakers, in the pitch of the whitecaps, she saw what looked like a swimmer, face and arms cockle-shell white, swimming hard and sure like an Olympian, then flailing, tumbling, pulled by a current parallel to the surf. Leigh ran across the hard-packed sand, keeping her eye on the roofline of the house, on her destination, not looking into the surf, not looking back.

A little swirl of tide encircled her ankle like a cold hand and tripped her. She fell prostrate, and the next wave rushed up in a cold gritty swash to her waist, then retreated, pulling her toward the surf. She tried to bring herself to her knees. The cold wet sand sucked at her clothes, her body. A wave rushed up to her chest, knocked her down again. The water filled her mouth, covered her head. The hand, now strong as a shackle, clenched tighter around her ankle. Her face was turned to the next wave of oncoming water. "I'm sorry!" she said into her fists, coughing, strangling. "I'm sorry I was young and stupid! And cruel!"

Her ankle was released—or was it just the retreat of the wave? She pried herself up from the cold wet beach. Choking, eyes and throat stinging, shivering from the wet cold, her clothes heavy, she ran down the beach. She dreaded the cold hand that might any minute clasp her ankle, clutch her shoulder. She wanted to look back. She knew if she turned and saw nothing but the moonlit stretch of beach, the pounding surf, she could owe it all to her conscience, do some kind of penance, save herself nightmares. But what if. . . ?

She ran, dragging her legs through the deep dry sand, stumbling up the steps. She ran across the endless boardwalk, the thunder of her feet against the boards louder now than the roar of the surf. She was so glad to see that Kayla had left the front-porch light on, had waited up, and was standing there, holding the screen door open for her.

The COMFORTER

July 21, 1861, Flat Rock, North Carolina
Dearest Lydia,

The servants are downstairs bustling about, putting out food and draping the parlor with black crepe. Soon I must go down and put on my bravest face for them and for my children.

Meanwhile, I am determined to complete my fortnightly correspondence with you, my youngest and dearest sister. Even the dreadful dream I had last night, even the news I received a few moments ago, will not prevent it. For we vowed long ago when we were little girls playing in the dovecote at Live Oaks that, though the earth be moved, we would not lose touch, we would never fail to tell each other of every trial and tribulation of our lives.

And of every trifle! In the interest of my sanity and yours, I have continued, as you have encouraged me, to write to you of the little things of our everyday lives here. I have told you of my frustrations when planning a ball here; such occasions are as rare in these mountains as hillbilly hoedowns are in Charleston. But I make do by keeping the house stocked with wine glasses and champagne and all that we need to entertain as we do back home. I am frustrated by the lack of fresh crab-meat and oysters, but the abundance of wild turkeys for pre-serve of fowl is some compensation. I did tell you, I believe, of my irritation at having to write to New York for one of the new, more comfortable corsets that are taken for granted by the ladies in Charleston, of how, when I received it, I gave thanks for mail delivery, without which I would be walking, standing, sitting in a perpetual pinch to this day!

And, oh! The Russian charlotte Mrs. Middleton served at her last fete! Did I tell you that her cook gave Elsie the recipe, but Elsie insists she left something out, on purpose, of course? I have told you of every leisurely drive we've taken along Little River Road, of every picnic we've spread out over granite outcroppings, of our outings to Rock Creek Falls, of moonlit hikes to Glassy Rock.

I have some serious concerns as well. With Mr. Alston and Jeremiah away at battle, the children sorely try me. Though Melanie favors you more every year, and has your (her favorite aunt) gentle, compassionate ways, she has shown an alarming penchant for courting danger. The other day I caught her huddled under a stand of hemlocks near our house here, rehearsing the alphabet with the laundress's children! Young James is just as incorrigible in his own way. He shuns the planned picnics and play parties and sneaks away with the kitchen boy to roam the forests in pursuit of bobcats and timber rattlers. How he needs the gentlemanly influence of his father and brother! How we all need this war to end!

Oh, Lydia, it seems that everything I have to tell you, even news of the children, is mindless drivel compared to the tidings that your letters bring to me as you tend to our wounded on the battlefield. Your accounts of soldiers grievously wounded, some screaming for God's mercy as they endure amputation of limbs, never leave my mind. Though you mercifully stopped writing to me of those things when I told you that the men of my own household had joined the infantry, I cannot get the images out of my mind. And I can never forget your account of the soldier who spoke to you with his last dying breath, warning you to guard your own safety near the battlefield, your own health in the fetid Lowcountry climate. How bittersweet that in this dying man you may have found your soul's mate at last.

And to think that I had the impudence, in my last letter, to complain of our grueling two-week trek from the Lowcountry to our summer colony here in North Carolina's Blue Ridge Mountains! To think I have complained that I must pack up the family and all the servants to flee the Lowcountry heat and the threat of the malarial fever every year. I should be thankful that we have such a splendid retreat to come to, that we have the health, the stamina, to withstand the arduous journey. Here, far away from the fever and the battlefield, it is shameful how easy it is to forget our good fortune.

Yet, still, "our ancient foe" who seeks "to work us woe" does not altogether avoid our doorsteps. While we dance and smile and sip Madeira and nibble bonbons and Italian crèmes, we cannot know from one moment to the next whether father, son, husband, brother lies mangled on some battlefield. Deserters from our own cause camp out in the mountains nearby ready to pillage our homes. Only last week a neighbor of ours, the finest of gentlemen, was shot in his own home by bushwhackers.

And whatever respite from grief and sickness our mountain retreat might seem to offer us, it is short-lived. Whenever we return to the Lowcountry in November we will meet with sad news. It is inevitable, as you know. Our first order of business when we arrive will be to find out who died of the fever during our absence.

But even now, in these momentous times, we must keep each other abreast about the smallest, most ordinary events of each day. So I shall go right ahead and proclaim, even at this grim time, how much I miss beautiful, bustling Charleston and all the plans that are now being made for the Saint Cecilia Ball, all the fuss over decor, menus, entertainment! How I pine for our walks along the Battery with salt spray in our faces! How my senses are starved for the narrow, walled gardens resplendent with wisteria and jessamine!

But it is lovely here, as well. Lydia, I do regret that, because Papa sent you to Europe during most fever seasons and to finishing schools in Boston the rest of the time, you have not been here with us since you were quite young. Do you remember how the air is here, how cool, how astringent? I am tempted to believe it must indeed be a cure, not only for the fever which we come here to escape, but for every disease that afflicts mankind! And do you recall the view from my window here by the English writing desk I salvaged from our old Tradd Street residence? The mile-long drive leads through tall trees to the road. It is a fetching sight; I have not tired of it yet. I believe it was you who pointed out that it is not unlike the live oak allée at Boone Hall, although the trees here are hemlocks, and beneath them mountain laurels with thick leathery leaves bloom like giant roses this time of year. Beyond, the high hills of the Blue Ridge undulate like blue waves in a choppy sea, with Mount Pisgah in the distance.

Lydia, do you remember how, as children, we used to walk along the Battery in our beloved Charleston, with our other siblings in tow, often with a storm out at sea and the waves crashing over the walls? I remember thinking on one of those occasions, when our girlish banter had slowed for the moment, that nothing could turn our thoughts toward God as did a storm along the Battery. But every year when I see again these sprawling vistas culminating in high blue hills, I have to say that nothing on this earth stirs my soul as does a long-range view toward a great height!

But now, as I write, I am brought down from the pinnacle of my musings by the clatter of crystal and silver in the parlor. The funereal drone of the servants' voices reminds me that tonight I must have the seamstress tuck in my black frock and press the creases out of my veil; tomorrow I will glide down the stairway with the seamless grace all women of our station must master by adulthood. I will greet my guests when they arrive, hold my head up and my hands out, eager to accept and to give solace.

I will pick up my cross when I am able. But, for now, I have only one ambition: to complete what I have started here. To stave off my grief by going on as if my life had not changed forever. Though my hand quivers so much that my penmanship is poor, my task will not be complete until I've told you all that has transpired on this sad day.

Early in the morning I awoke, or dreamed I awoke, just in time to see a white dove fly slowly from the open window, across the room. It alighted first on the bedpost and then on the headboard, where it stayed for a moment. Then it disappeared from my sight altogether. We all know that a white dove alighting on the bedpost signifies death, that the dove, that ancient symbol of peace, is sent as a warning, to comfort us before the greatest of trials.

Immediately, in that loneliest hour of the night, Mr. Matthew Brady's photographs from the battlefield arose in my mind: soldiers maimed or killed in battle, dying in makeshift hospitals. My mind, with the awful clarity that we have on just waking, cruelly placed the faces of my husband, my son Jeremiah, and our sister's son Daniel in those awful scenes. I cursed the day I saw the photographs in all their startling reality. I thought of all the forlorn and dreary homes to which father, brother, husband, son will never return. That not only our summer home here in these mountains, but lovely Live Oaks in the blessed Lowcountry would soon know such sorrow! I felt a surge of bitterness that whatever news I would have to hear, you, my youngest, dearest sister, would not be here to help me bear it.

With such images crowding my mind, I could not hope to sleep. I was determined that, until I heard the news that was sure to come, I would live every moment as if all were well. And so, by the glow of a single lamp augmenting the gray light of dawn, I steeled myself, took out pen and parchment, and made ready to write to you about all that had happened since my last letter. I would write to you as if all were well, believing that all would indeed be well, until the precise moment I was forced to learn otherwise.

So much to tell! The thoughts flooded my mind so swiftly I could not decide where to start. I knew I should tell you all about the services at Mr. Baring's chapel. I knew I should reiterate his messages, which are generally thoughtful, if never stirring. I knew I should quote the passages of Scripture he used, tell you which hymns were sung. But wicked me! I itched to tell you of last night's fete at Mrs. Barnwell's, how beautifully her servant band performed, how exquisite was the boned pheasant with truffles, how such sharp looks passed between the two Misses Pinckneys when Mr. Rhett came into the ballroom, resplendent in his Confederate uniform! I thought about how to describe to you their demeanor, how brightly both young ladies smiled as they danced the quadrille, all the while looking as if they could spew venom at each other! How the mountain trout our hostess served was delicious, though no substitute for the crab pâté everyone serves at such gatherings in the Lowcountry, or for shrimp harvested straight from the briny deep!

But I had not yet put pen to paper when I heard the slow clip-clop, clip-clop of horse hooves making their way down the drive. Finally they slowed to a stop at the carriage circle.

It is unusual to have a guest at such an hour, and because of the dream I thought the worst. I remembered that a neighbor had sent one of his coachman's stableboys to Asheville as an emissary to camp outside the telegraph office. There he would await news from the battlefront. If—Heaven forbid!—he received news of casualties, he would report the sad findings to my neighbor, who would then assume the dread task of getting the news to the bereaved family. My first thought was that this stableboy messenger, or my neighbor himself, had arrived with news for me.

But here, alas, is the strange thing: I did not jump up and run downstairs to find out. I did not even stand up from my seat and part the curtains to look down. I only listened to the subdued mumbles as the messenger, whoever he was, talked to our man Silas in the carriage circle. I heard Silas ask the messenger what news he brought. I tried to assure myself that the news might not be so dire. For there is something in the human spirit that feels as long as we don't know that all is not well, there is still reason for hope.

And, strangely, at just that moment I felt you here, Lydia! I remembered an incident that occurred two years ago at Live Oaks. I was at ease in the parlor finishing a piece of fancy-work. Though we were not expecting you, though I had not heard the approach of your carriage or the knock on the door, some inaudible voice whispered to me, "Look up! Look up!" I looked up and there you stood, in the middle of the room, regarding me with sadness and concern. You, or your image, promptly vanished. Hours later you arrived to tell me that our mother had died of the fever. Do you see, Lydia? Even before you were able to reach me with the news of mother's death, you were there in spirit, as if you had come ahead along some astral thoroughfare to comfort me before you had to break the news to me face-to-face!

And so you did this very morning. Just as the messenger broke the news to Silas below my window, I heard a rustle of crinoline as someone rushed across the floor toward me! When I turned my head to see who it might be, I saw both of our reflections in the tall mirror by the bureau. I saw myself leaning over the desk with pen to parchment. My reflection watched as you stood over me, your comforting hand resting on my shoulder. Then you were gone as suddenly as the dove had gone, and I was left looking at my own bewildered face. Just as last night's dream had come to forewarn and to comfort me, so had you.

I sat for some time, pondering what I had seen. I wondered if this sympathetic erasure of time and space is not uncommon between women who are as close in spirit as you and I have always been.

Someone knocked at the door. I did not answer. I leaned forward on the desk and held my face in both hands.

"Missus!" Charity called softly. I did not answer. "Missus!" she said again, knocking hard on my door.

"Alright, Charity," I said, finally. "Come in, if you must." But as she entered, though my heart beat fast with anticipation, I forbade her to tell me the reason she had come. I put up my hand and shook my head as she was about to speak. I could not bear to look at that wretchedly sad face. "Go back downstairs, Charity, and tell the messenger that I will meet him within the hour."

"But Missus—" she said. Her face wrenched. She wrung her hands.

"I know, Charity. I know you have news to tell." But, whatever the news, she need not tell me, not yet; I would not hear it, not yet!

Clearly, the poor girl could not fathom my attitude. Nor could I. Surely any other wife, mother, sister, daughter of a soldier at war would hang on every thread of news, truth, rumor, or falsehood that came from the battlefield; surely no one but I could have forborne the servant girl's knowing news that I did not, news that was mine, that would change my life utterly and forever. I have no doubt that the vacant look of disbelief in Charity's eyes was but a reflection of the same look in mine. I know now that I was, for that moment and the few moments that followed, truly deranged.

"Do as I am about to tell you," I said. Then I proceeded to give her the ludicrous instructions: "Go back downstairs, Charity. Ask Hannah to prepare for the guests who will start arriving tomorrow. You know what to do. Make sure the silver is polished, get out our best Madeira. And," I could not believe my own words, "put the wreath on the door. I'll be down within the hour to supervise the other arrangements."

Oh, did her eyes grow wide at that! "Yes'm," she said, shaking her head as she backed out of the room, with that inimitable show of disbelief at which servants are so gifted.

And so once again I started to write, but dropped my pen as I heard, outside my door, Charity's voice mingled with my dear daughter Melanie's subdued sobs. Melanie knew and was coming to me for comfort. The weight would be dropped on my shoulders whether or not I was ready to bear it.

"Come in," I said, when the two women approached my door. The door opened. Charity stood there, her eyes moist with tears. And there stood Melanie, the very picture of you, Lydia, overcome with grief over the loss of her cousin? Brother? Father? I could no longer forestall hearing the truth, now that my daughter knew. Charity looked at her feet, and then Melanie told me.

The messenger who had come was not a neighbor's servant with news from the battlefield. It was Elias, the son of our foreman at Live Oaks. Elias had been sent across the miles to tell me.

Charity came to my side and helped me sit again. She ran to the washstand and came back with a cool cloth for my forehead. Melanie knelt by my side and gave in to sobs. I lay my hand on her head and stroked her chestnut hair as I had yours, Lydia, the night you told me that your Mr. Drayton had asked another's hand in marriage, and that you would not risk such heartbreak again, but would instead dedicate your life to the service of others.

After a moment Melanie looked up at me, at the writing desk, then back at me again. "You were writing to her?" she asked, incredulously. I nodded. Wise girl that Melanie is, she looked at me and understood that I would complete the letter to you, even now. For haven't I always shared all things with my dear sister, all things? After a moment I begged them to leave me, assuring them I was quite alright. They left reluctantly, softly closing the door behind them.

So I was again left with my place here at the writing desk. I stubbornly kept writing to you even after learning the news. And now . . . and now? Oh, Lydia! I would commit my own soul to eternal torment if I could have persuaded you to come here with us to escape the fever. I would ask you to come again as you did no less than an hour ago to comfort me, but I know that for me to ask is selfish and for you to comply may be impossible. Your soul has flown now; I can feel it. The room is now as empty of your spirit as if you had never been born. How I envy your peace that passes all understanding.

I will sign this letter and seal it with wax, as I always do. I will have Silas take it to the post, as always. It is strange and yet comforting to think that all the letters we have written over the years might be found, long after I too am gone, in a trunk of the dusty attic at Live Oaks, yellowed and severed at the folds, a minuscule record of the everyday lives of two sisters, two kindred souls. I like to think that as much as a century from now someone might read how two sisters, as children, built villas out of sand at Pawley's Island, how they hunted salamanders in the creeks of the Blue Ridge Mountains, how as young women they fussed over plans for fetes, complained over having to wear corsets, how they exulted and cried over loves won and lost.

I have heard that a fragment of broken crockery can tell an archeologist as much about a past civilization as the whole of the Parthenon. I like to think that the letters we have written may be like that, that they will somehow find their place among other inevitable artifacts of our time, like a set of combs and brushes, a tarnished rice spoon, a coin dug from the earth where a proud soldier fell. I like to think that someday someone will find in the heartfelt letters between long-dead sisters a telling record of the small grievances and the small glories of their passing days, that they will find in them a small fragment of the greater testimony of our time.

ANGEL *Unawares*

Faye had always looked after her Aunt Vaughtie, even before the drifter came to town. Aunt Vaughtie had once called Faye her guardian angel, but Faye had dismissed the angel part. She knew that a genuine angel would not resent being the only one in the family to worry about and look after her elderly, widowed aunt. An angel wouldn't despise Aunt Vaughtie's sorry son, Roy, for never coming to visit his mother or for never getting around to fixing up things around her house. Faye knew she was no angel, though she had always done what she could for Aunt Vaughtie, even though she had a job and her own house and yard to take care of, even though she lived an hour and fifteen minutes away.

Faye worried all the time about Aunt Vaughtie. She worried because the doctor said that Vaughtie's mild strokes might be warnings of a massive one to come. She worried Vaughtie would step out on the front porch stoop in the winter, slip on the ice, and break a hip. She worried about her driving the curvy mountain roads with one eye clouded from a cataract. Mainly, though, she worried about Vaughtie's blindness when it came to people. It was as if the part of her brain where caution and skepticism reside had been removed before her birth.

Faye was just the opposite. She always had her eyes wide open, knew what could happen in this ugly world, and couldn't pretend she didn't. So many times she had intercepted Aunt Vaughtie before she handed over cash to men who promised to fix holes in her roof that weren't even there, or sent checks to slick, pompadoured televangelists.

But most of all it worried Faye that, even though a woman

who lived alone not two miles away had been robbed at gunpoint in her kitchen, Aunt Vaughtie refused to keep her doors locked and was way too friendly with strangers. Faye had talked to Aunt Rose about it, but Rose said that was just the way Vaughtie was, the way she always had been, and frankly, Rose said, she envied Vaughtie's bright outlook.

Faye had tried to talk to Roy about installing motion-detector lights outside and trimming down some of that jungle growth of red-tip photinias in the backyard, where criminals could so easily hide. Instead he had brought over a figure he had cut out of half-inch plywood. It was painted black and shaped like a Rottweiler. He had set it up against Aunt Vaughtie's chain-link fence, and Aunt Vaughtie had honestly believed, as Roy had told her, that the silhouette would deter burglars. Faye even tried to get a neighborhood watch program started in Aunt Vaughtie's community, but hardly anybody came to the meetings. Nobody paid Faye any mind, not even Aunt Vaughtie. "Faye, you just always think of the worst," she would say.

But the Saturday morning the drifter came to town, it seemed, even to Faye, like nothing bad had ever happened, or could ever happen, in the world. It was warm for a late morning in spring, and breezy. The rolling East Tennessee foothills had started greening up all around; alabaster clouds sailed across a baby-blue sky, and the dogwoods were starting to bloom in the woods around Aunt Vaughtie's lovely green acre. Faye, pear-shaped, ponytailed, and sweating, and Aunt Vaughtie, a birdy little woman under a broad-brimmed straw hat, were down on their knees pulling up the pansies and planting red salvia in a patch of sunny ground outside Vaughtie's house. The pansies hadn't even become leggy yet and it was too early to plant annuals, but Vaughtie wanted it done. Faye knew if she didn't help her, Vaughtie would do it herself and get down in the back.

Toward noon they heard music blasting from a radio. Boom boom. Boom boom boom. Gravel rattled in the driveway, and Faye craned her neck around to see a man driving up in a rust bucket of a truck. That *boom boom* by itself was enough to turn

Faye against the driver before she even saw his face. The truck stopped just three feet short of Faye's upturned behind. When the man who was driving stepped out of the truck, she recognized him on the spot. She had seen him in town at the corner of Fifth and Church streets. He had been slouched on the tailgate of that same truck, and had been holding a sign that said WILL WORK FOR FOOD. To Faye he was the picture of trouble. He had long graying hair under a ball cap, a sleeveless, threadbare shirt, and psychedelic tattoos on his skinny arms. His gray locks blew a little in the wind, like Spanish moss. "You ladies got any odd jobs need doing?" he asked.

He had left the truck going and the radio playing. Boom boom boom. Boom boom boom. Faye stood up, with some effort, and wiped her hands on her pedal pushers. "I can't hear you," she said, even though she could. The man raised his eyebrows in response to her sarcastic tone. He kept his eyes hard on her as he slowly reached in the truck and switched off the ignition. Silence.

"Name's Ace," he said, holding out his big dirty hand. Faye grabbed Aunt Vaughtie's hand before she could reach out to shake his. Ace put his hands into his pockets and leaned back against the door of the truck. "What I said was: 'You ladies got anything needs doing around here?'"

Aunt Vaughtie, who'd always prided herself in looking past appearances straight to the heart, shoved back her wide-brimmed hat and beamed a smile like she'd just won the lottery. "Why, I've got no end of things that need fixing!" she said, before Faye had a chance to elbow her in the ribs. "My gutters need cleaning. The chimney needs sweeping. There's painting to be done. How much do you charge?"

"Not a thing, ma'am," he said. "I'll be happy to work just for food."

"Well!" Aunt Vaughtie said. "That certainly sounds like a bargain! And it's been a long time since I've had the pleasure of cooking for a man!"

Ace grinned, showing one gold tooth. "I'm not particular, either," he said. He patted his stomach. "I don't care what you fix, just fix plenty of it." He said it as if they'd already struck a deal and he were in the position to call the shots. That riled Faye.

"We don't need any help, thank you," she said. "My husband and I take care of what needs doing around here." Vaughtie slid her eyes toward her niece. Faye's husband, a man much older than Faye, had been dead for going on seven years.

Ace's eyes said he knew Faye was bluffing. He looked at the ground, chewed his lips to disguise his grin. "Well, if you don't mind me saying so, from the looks of things around here, your husband could use some help. You talk it over with him. I'll stop back by this way in a day or two."

"That won't be necessary," Faye said, her voice shaking. Ace hopped in the truck, then leaned his head out the window and grinned, showing his gold tooth. Faye's heart beat like a drum.

Before he'd had time to back out of the driveway, Aunt Vaughtie scolded Faye. "Now why did you have to lie and say all that about a husband?"

"Because, Aunt Vaughtie! A man like that does not need to know you live here by yourself!" They were back down on the ground planting again. Faye's fingers trembled as she untangled the roots at the bottom of a plant.

"Oh, he was alright!" Vaughtie said, gleefully pulling another tray of salvia toward her. "Did you see how skinny he was? Why, I could fatten him up good just on what I throw away after supper!" Faye shook her head. "A handyman who'll work just for food!" Vaughtie said. "With me on a fixed income and all. It's an answer to a prayer!"

"I've always heard you should be careful what you pray for," Faye said. "Or you just might get it."

"Now, Faye!" Vaughtie replied.

Faye was afraid for her Aunt. She stayed overnight, as she often did, and took Aunt Vaughtie to Sunday school, church, and to the cafeteria for lunch. She wished she could stay all week, but she'd used all her vacation time and sick leave taking Aunt Vaughtie to doctors. Before she left Sunday afternoon, Faye held Aunt Vaughtie by her boney little shoulders, looked her straight in the eyes, and asked her for the second time if she wouldn't come stay with her for a few days.

"Oh, pooh!" Aunt Vaughtie said. "You know I can't sleep well in any bed but my own, and you know how I like to get my bath in time to watch the Montel show at four. And what would I do all day with you away at work? I'm staying right here!"

"Alright then, but please, Aunt Vaughtie, keep your doors locked. And if that man comes back, please don't give him the time of day." Aunt Vaughtie turned her head and did a quick little nod that meant she'd do just as she pleased.

All the next week, as Faye worked at her job at the credit union in Knoxville and tended her own house and yard, the man named Ace scuttled like a gray tumbleweed across the back of her mind. She called Aunt Vaughtie first thing Monday morning, and again at nine that night, just before Aunt Vaughtie fell asleep watching the Inspirational Network, as she usually did. "You locked all the doors, right?" she asked Aunt Vaughtie. "And the phone is right by the bed?" When she called Tuesday night, Faye asked her if Ace had ever come back.

"Hmm," Aunt Vaughtie said. Faye knew that could mean yes or no, and probably meant yes. Faye called a man she knew who owned a hardware store in Oak Ridge and paid for him to drive out to Aunt Vaughtie's and install double-key deadbolt locks on the doors and motion-detector lights over the back porch. Faye called to remind Aunt Vaughtie that the locks were no good unless she used them, and to close her mini-blinds at night, too. She could tell that her doting was starting to get on Aunt Vaughtie's nerves and was making no inroads into her rose-garden mind, so she stopped calling so much. But she bit her fingernails, hardly slept at night, and was foggy headed during the day at work.

On Friday Faye managed to get off work early so she could rush to Aunt Vaughtie's. As soon as she drove up she noticed that old pickup truck in the driveway, and she saw Ace down the hill by the creek pruning the branches of the rhododendrons. Faye ran into the kitchen.

"Now just unruffle those feathers!" Aunt Vaughtie said before Faye could say anything. "Ace came by just as he promised, and he said borers are eating up the rhododendrons and they ought to be trimmed back, and he'd be glad to do it for me in exchange for a light lunch." She wouldn't look at Faye. She was busy lifting a pot lid and spooning mounds of creamed potatoes onto a china plate.

Faye lifted the lid of another pot and looked in. "You made him beef tips for lunch?" she said, unbelieving.

"Well, he said he didn't much care for sandwiches, and this was all I had in the freezer."

Faye glared at her. "I thought he said he wasn't particular." She lifted the lid of another pot and there, swimming in big dollops of melting butter, lay the very last of the green lima beans she had helped Vaughtie plant, pick, shell, and freeze last summer. That had been a lot of work, and Aunt Vaughtie knew that baby limas were Faye's favorite, but here she was letting this strange man eat them up. She let Aunt Vaughtie know how she felt about it, too.

"Well, if you knew all he'd done around here, you'd agree with me that it is more than fair payment!" Aunt Vaughtie said. Ace had painted the wrought iron around the patio, she said, and the metal roof of the well house. He had cleaned the gutters and the chimney and had poured kerosene down into the yellow jacket nests under the apple trees. And next he was going to chop down all that awful sweet-pea vine that had taken over the split-rail fence.

In a little while the great Ace, all smirk and swagger, walked into the kitchen. Faye nodded coolly, and Aunt Vaughtie, beaming, handed him a plate piled with food. He didn't say a thing, just shoveled in the food, cutting his eyes toward Faye like a dog warning another to stay clear. He licked his plate when he was done, eyeing Faye over the rim. It made her sick.

"I just can't tell you how it warms my heart to see a man eat like that," Aunt Vaughtie said, watching him.

"Be back early in the morning," he said. "Get started on that sweet-pea vine first thing." Dread covered Faye like a wave. Boom boom boom. The rattletrap truck drove away.

Aunt Vaughtie stood at the sink, happily washing the dirty dishes. Faye took her by the shoulders and swung her around. Soap suds whirled from Aunt Vaughtie's fingertips. Her eyes were wide, scared. "Aunt Vaughtie, think," Faye said. "Think! Why would a man do that much work just for food? Can't you see that he is bound to have some plan, some plot, some ulterior motive?"

"Oh, Faye! Like what?"

"Alright," Faye said. She stood right in Aunt Vaughtie's face, practically pinning her against the kitchen sink. "At the very least he could be befriending you just to gain your trust. Then, once he's suckered you good, he'll hit you up for money. Or he could be planning to come in and rob you. Or—and remember, Aunt Vaughtie, these things do happen, and not just in the movies—he could be planning to creep into the house at night and strangle you to death!"

"Oh, Faye!" Aunt Vaughtie fell back against the kitchen sink and put her wet hands to her cheeks. "Have you gone through the menopause yet, Faye? Have you been taking your estrogen tablets regular?"

"Aunt Vaughtie, I don't like this."

"The trouble with you, sugar, is you have no faith. You know what the Bible says: 'Do not be afraid to entertain strangers, for thereby some have entertained angels unawares.'"

"In this case," Faye said, "you're just as likely to be entertaining the Devil."

"Oh, now, Faye!" Aunt Vaughtie turned and shook her head and kept on washing the dishes.

"I'm staying the night," Faye said, and she did. She went through the house and triple checked all the locks on the doors and windows. She barely slept. Before sunup the smell of fried bacon and coffee wafted into her room and she thought she heard whispers. Aunt Vaughtie ate Grape Nuts every morning, so why then did she smell bacon? She dragged herself into the front of the house, sleepless and groggy.

Nothing could have prepared her for the spectacle of Ace and Aunt Vaughtie having breakfast together, not in the kitchen, but in the dining room. The white company cloth was

spread over the oval table. What must have been two pounds
of bacon, a dozen eggs, biscuits, and enough grits to feed the
National Guard had been served up in Vaughtie's best china
dishes. Her old silver service, ornate and recently polished, sat
in the middle of the table. As Faye entered, Aunt Vaughtie
was pouring Ace a cup of steaming coffee from the gilded pot.
Worst of all, Aunt Vaughtie was dressed in her finest lavender
gown and robe set. She had made a clumsy effort at teasing
her hair, and with the visual aid of her one good eye she had
smeared fuchsia lipstick on her little slit of a mouth. She sat
there looking like a fairy godmother on a drunk. All she
needed was a tiara. "Aunt Vaughtie!"

Vaughtie jumped. Ace took one look at Faye, wiped his
mouth with a cloth napkin, grinned behind it, and made a
show of folding it fastidiously and laying it on his plate. He
stood up, swaggered to the kitchen, and washed up at the sink
with the easy familiarity of the man of the house. Aunt Vaughtie, frowning, handed him a dish towel. He took it and dried
his hands.

"You couldn't have had enough to eat Ace!"

He nodded. "My appetite took a sudden turn," he said. "I'll
just go on and get started trimming that sweet-pea vine."

Faye grabbed her purse and followed Ace out to the yard.
"Faye! What are you doing?" Aunt Vaughtie cried.

Faye followed Ace all the way up the hill to the fence.
"What does it take?" she asked, running to catch up to him.
He stopped, kept his back turned toward her, his hands in his
pockets. She pulled a wad of cash out of her purse and flashed
it in his face. Her hands and voice trembled. "What does it
take to get you to go away from here and never come back—
ever?"

He looked at Faye and grinned, flashed his gold tooth.
"Ever? Now, that's a mighty tall order." He shook his gray
head at the money. "Never mind that," he said. "I'll collect
by and by." He dropped the hedge shears at his feet and
ambled off toward his truck. He jumped in the seat, started
the engine, and turned the radio up as loud as it would go.
BOOM BOOM BOOM! He backed out, and Aunt Vaughtie,

who had been watching from the screen porch, came running out, flopping her apron in agitation, waving him down, calling out, "Ace! Oh, Ace!" Aunt Vaughtie stood in the driveway and wiped a tear from her eye with the tail of her apron. "Faye, I could just pinch you for running him off! Don't you know how hard it is to get a man who will do odd jobs? And for practically free?"

"Aunt Vaughtie he—"

"Oh, Faye, I know you mean well, but sometimes you interfere too much. Sometimes I wish you would just mind your own business!" Aunt Vaughtie's eyes widened at the force of her words. "Oh!" she squeaked, and put her fingers to her lips.

"Alright, Aunt Vaughtie," Faye said, and walked to the house to gather up her things.

Vaughtie grabbed Faye's arm to hold her back, then followed her into the house. "Oh, Faye, dear! Please forgive me for what I just said. Don't you understand that I am more afraid of being afraid than of anything that man, or anybody else, could do to me? I'm not as stupid as I act. Do you honestly think I could get through eighty years without knowing there's evil in the world, and that evil can come right to my doorstep? But refusing to live with fear is how I've managed to live through eighty years with such a sunny disposition!"

"Alright, Aunt Vaughtie," Faye said again. Vaughtie followed her through the house as she gathered up her things and made ready to go. "Maybe you're right," Faye said, wearily. "Maybe I have been interfering. But as of today, I just wipe my hands of it, Aunt Vaughtie. I will just have to accept that I can't be your protector any more than a mother can protect her child."

Aunt Vaughtie cried. Faye kissed her on the forehead, tossed her bag into the car, and drove away. "Oh, Faye! Faye!" Aunt Vaughtie called after her.

But Faye didn't look back. She drove home, went to bed, and slept like the dead. Late the next morning Faye was awakened by Aunt Vaughtie's voice calling for her. "Faye! Oh, Faye!" Faye shot up, surprised she was in her own bed, in her own home, not at Aunt Vaughtie's. It was as if Aunt Vaughtie were calling her from the next room. "Faye!"

She jumped into her clothes, then jumped into the car and sped along the highway to Aunt Vaughtie's, her heart skipping beats, her foot hard on the pedal. "Faye!" She heard her aunt's voice just as plain as if Vaughtie were in the backseat, right there in the car. The green hills swooshed by her as she sped down the road.

Half a dozen cars were parked in Aunt Vaughtie's driveway. Men stood around, their faces grave. Ace was back. He was parking cars like an old family friend who knew how to stay in the background and be of some use in a crisis. He saw Faye, nodded. Gertie Brown waddled up the steps to the house carrying the chess pie she brought to every occasion.

Aunt Vaughtie? Faye ran toward the screen porch, where people were gathered around Vaughtie, who sat small as a doll in her wicker chair. She had her face in her hands. A dozen or more people rallied around her. Her son Roy was among them.

"What happened?" Faye asked one sober face, then another. "Aunt Vaughtie?"

"Who's that hoodlum out there?" Bill Butler said, nodding toward Ace. "One of those bums who come to strangers' wakes and funerals just to get to eat?"

"I reckon that's just that hired hand she's been bragging so much about," Roy said. "Hired man or handyman, or whatever it is you call him."

"Hired hand," Faye said. "Hired man, handyman. Death Angel. Somehow I knew it all along."

"Oh, Aunt Vaughtie, you won't believe what I saved you from this time," she said, though her aunt didn't hear.

Nobody heard. She ran from Gertie Brown to Aunt Rose to Bill Butler to Cousin Roy. She ran from one to the other of them as they arrived: family, neighbors, preacher. She talked right in their faces, trying to warn them, trying to get them to understand, but not a one of them paid her a bit of mind.

The Other WOMAN

On her bedroom dresser in her big stucco house in the swanky suburbs north of Atlanta, Lou Ellen kept a small white porcelain hand she had bought on a whim years before at a flea market. The hand sat straight up on its wrist like a tree on its trunk, and around its curving, upturned fingers she kept her favorite gemstone rings. She kept a string of pearls, a diamond pendant, and two thin gold chains draped across the palm, from the hand's thumb to its delicate pinky finger.

Her husband, George, was away on business most of the time. One night Lou Ellen, alone in her big house, woke up sure somebody had been in her bedroom, though when she eased up in bed and opened her eyes she didn't see a soul. On her dresser the milky-white, tapered fingers caught the streetlight, and she could tell, even from several feet away, that somebody had toyed with her rings, had rearranged them like Chinese checkers, and had let her necklaces fall in a shimmery puddle around the base of the wrist.

Her eyes slid from corner to shadowed corner of the semi-darkened room. She was silent for a long time. "Jill?" she whispered. But of course there was no answer. She knew that her former housekeeper had a key to the house, though Jill, being dead, would hardly need a key to enter. She fell back in bed, and lay there like a board for the rest of the night, wishing for morning to come.

In the morning she made an appointment with a therapist.

Lou Ellen had been what some people might call haunted for most of her fifty-seven years. If she was haunted and her older relatives in the north Georgia mountains had known about it, they would say she sure got it honest. Many of her forebears, especially her great-grandmother Maud Harmon, were said to have had second sight. From the Harmon branch of her family, Lou Ellen had grown up hearing that crows landing on rooftops foretold deaths in the family. Granny Maud herself used to say words over warts to make them go away. Her own great-grandfather had seen blood on the moon, and afterward the Ellijay River had flooded, washing away houses, barns, and gristmills, whisking away in its terrible tide even the dead in their caskets.

Lou Ellen's great-aunt Cora was the one who kept those stories alive by getting the older Harmons to talk them up at the reunions. They didn't have the Harmon family reunions anymore, because the older ones had died off and so many of the younger ones had moved down to Atlanta or farther away for jobs. But they used to have them every August at the old homeplace in Gilmer County. At those gatherings they would mainly talk about who was sick or down in the back, who had died, who had to have a shotgun wedding, things like that. The musicians among them would pick and grin some. They'd play cards and kickball. The kids would play by the creek or run off to pick blackberries in the woods, and come back covered with ticks.

But toward sundown, when some of the group started to think about heading home, Aunt Cora—the one who made the family tree and kept albums with pictures of everybody as far back as pictures were made—always got them talking about the old times. "Arnold, tell them the one about the empty grave," she'd say. Pretty soon one storyteller would try to best the next one, so you never had a clue what might be true from what was made up on the spot.

Aunt Cora herself liked to tell a tale, and she told it for the truth. One moonless summer night in 1862, her own great-grandmother, a young woman then, had been walking home from helping a neighbor woman birth a baby, when she'd seen her own daddy walking along the road. His Confederate uniform was aglow like foxfire, and he passed right by her, his eyes firmly fixed on something far off. Later on they found out he'd been killed more than a month earlier at the Battle of

Seven Days in Virginia.

Water runs downhill, Aunt Cora used to say, so it stood to reason that somebody somewhere down the Harmon family line would have what they called "the sight." They would believe Lou Ellen was the one, too, if she'd ever told anybody what all she'd seen. She had seen plenty in her time, and it had started early. There was the face in the pond at a family reunion. Then there was the time when she was in third, or maybe fourth, grade. She was sitting at her desk in the schoolroom and was bored with the arithmetic problem the teacher was drawing out on the blackboard. She was overcome with the urge to look out the window, and when she did she saw a little girl swinging at the playground. The girl, who wore a jacket with a pointed hood, waved to her, then swung high and reckless, showing off, just the way Charlotte Watkins, the classmate who had died over summer vacation, used to do. But Lou Ellen knew she had no reason whatsoever to believe that little imp, whoever she was, was Charlotte Watkins. At recess the little girl was gone.

Haunted. She guessed she'd call it that, though she'd always thought haunted meant visited by the dead. Some of her visitants had not been dead, not that she knew of. When Lou Ellen was in her twenties her father had died, and at the graveside service she'd seen a woman standing like an outcast at a distance from the family. This woman was dressed in black, and her face was half hidden by the heavy rain that fell like a veil off the edge of her black umbrella.

Was it one of her father's other women? There had been some, she knew, and Lou Ellen had watched how gracefully her mother had handled the many betrayals. Lou Ellen's mother, by her actions, had made it seem inevitable that all men would behave in such a way. When Lou Ellen found out about George's affairs, it was no big surprise to her. Lou Ellen had always felt that somebody was waiting around every darkened corner for her, somebody with no qualms whatsoever about moving in and taking over her life. So when the other women surfaced it confirmed her suspicions. But who was that woman standing in the graveyard, stubbornly separating herself from the rest of the mourners at her father's funeral, watching Lou Ellen through the gray distance? Whoever she was, her steady gaze had given Lou Ellen a chill she couldn't owe to the occasion or the wet weather.

But all those episodes—and there were more—came months, sometimes years apart. In between times, Lou Ellen was able to file them away as minor mysteries. But she had been unable to put out of her mind the little incidents that had occurred following the death of her latest housekeeper, Jill, with whom George had been carrying on an affair. Lou Ellen knew that Jill, unlike her other mysterious visitants, was most definitely dead, and she knew that Jill might blame her, Lou Ellen, for her death. So, naturally, when George was away, which was most of the time, and Lou Ellen was alone in the quiet hours in the big empty house, when she heard the click of heels on the Italian tile floor or found that the jewelry on her dainty porcelain glove mold had been tampered with, she wondered if Jill might have come back to tease her a little. Or even to hold her accountable.

Lou Ellen had hired Jill not only because she had been recommended, but also because she had a strange face, with slightly upturned and flattened features. Jill didn't have the storybook prettiness that George seemed to favor, so Lou Ellen thought that maybe nothing would develop between them. She knew George had indulged in many affairs, and though she was adept at looking the other way, like her mother, she knew she could not tolerate it right under her nose, with someone she dealt with on a weekly basis.

Things had started out well enough. Jill came on time every Thursday, and she had the efficiency Lou Ellen would expect from an older, career housekeeper. Jill was the first maid who dusted the cobwebs off the ceiling fans and vacuumed under the sofa without being told. Lou Ellen was so impressed with her that she didn't mind that Jill made herself so much at home, that she organized the kitchen cabinets and the linen closets to suit herself, that she helped herself to the wine. Lou Ellen became friendly with Jill. She was trying to escape from a bad relationship and was having a hard time financially;

Lou Ellen listened to her troubles and paid her handsomely. They were nearly the same size and wore the same size shoes. They both had an affection for fine Italian leather. They became almost sisterly. Jill frequently borrowed Lou Ellen's jewelry, her shoes. With Lou Ellen's blessing, Jill often drove the Lexus, helped herself to the wine cellar. Before the first year was out, Lou Ellen found she had helped herself to George, too.

Lou Ellen, who had been brought up to act like a lady even when faced with such brazen betrayal, had kept her claws safely withdrawn until a Thursday between Christmas and New Year's. On that day there was a terrible ice storm, and the roads were a mess. George was home and had the TV on. There were accidents everywhere. Jill called to say that she guessed she ought to not drive in that weather, but Lou Ellen, wanting to bully her a little, insisted that she come. Their big New Year's Eve party was coming up, and she needed Jill to do this and that. Jill, who did not know Lou Ellen was wise to her dalliance with George, was bewildered by Lou Ellen's attitude. She protested; Lou Ellen insisted. They argued, although on Lou Ellen's side the argument remained low-key and ladylike throughout. Lou Ellen strongly suggested she might fire her and would see to it that Jill did not work again in the affluent north Atlanta suburbs. Jill finally, reluctantly, agreed to come.

When Jill didn't arrive in the usual thirty-five minutes, Lou Ellen was not surprised, because the roads were such a mess. She enjoyed the thought of Jill stuck in the difficult, slowed traffic, maybe involved in a little fender bender. But she never would have imagined that Jill would skid into a fallen tree two miles from her house and die at the scene. She hadn't wanted Jill to be killed. For a long time she felt like she would die herself, of guilt.

George, grief-stricken over Jill, went snowshoeing with friends in Manitoba.

During her first night alone in the big house after Jill's death, Lou Ellen heard footsteps downstairs in the wine cellar. The next night she heard the quick confident click of heels on her Italian tile floor. She lay stiff in bed, her eyes fixed to the tray ceiling. The next morning she'd found the front door ajar and damp footprints on the antique Persian rug in the foyer. Finally came the night the unseen visitor had tinkered with her jewelry.

She went to the therapist. "Sensory hallucinations, disintegration of personality brought on by recent stressors. . . ." This she read on her chart when the psychiatrist had to leave the room to answer an emergency phone call. When the doctor came back he prescribed an antianxiety drug and suggested a trip abroad or a change of environment.

Lou Ellen took the drug and the advice. She moved out of the grand house in the north Atlanta suburbs into their second home in the north Georgia mountains. She convinced herself that Jill wouldn't follow her there. She couldn't. What she thought was Jill had been nothing more than a shadow of her guilt; that's all it had been. She would put Jill out of her mind. She wouldn't say her name aloud and give her form. She would leave her there. Just before she left she heard hurried footsteps throughout the house, running up the steps, opening and closing closet doors. She closed and locked the door on Jill.

When she drove away from the house she looked back just in time to see the draperies in the great room part and fall closed again.

Lou Ellen moved into the log house that she and George had built on a wooded parcel of land that had been part of the old Harmon homestead. Her daddy had been a Harmon, and a great-uncle had inherited and held onto a good part of it, then had willed it to his son, who made most of it a conservation easement and sold off the remainder in parcels. Lou Ellen and George had bought a large tract of that land. There were no mountain views, but a level building site was hidden deep within the shade of old hemlocks.

They had built the house too big because they could so easily afford to. It had everything they had wanted—solid hickory floors, a huge two-sided stone fireplace open to the kitchen on one side and the great room on the other. In the great room a two-story picture window looked out over feathery hem-locks. A spiral staircase wound up to the second-floor loft, where there were two more bedrooms and the room George used for a study.

It was the day after Labor Day, and Lou Ellen's daughter, who had come to help her get settled, left to go back to Atlanta. The house was big and empty, too quiet. It was late afternoon, hot, and partly cloudy. That night would be her first night alone in the log house. But George was coming the next day. One night to get through, only one.

She thought a long walk might ease her nerves. She hoped it would exhaust her so sleep would come quickly that night. She put on snake boots and took a walk through the pine woods of the conservation easement. She trudged through thigh-high blackberry bushes and brambles to all that was left of Granny Maud's little cabin: a pile of rocks that had once been the chimney, the tin roof like a big book lying facedown over the collapsed timbers, the sweet bubby bushes Granny had grown beside her front-porch steps. She could just make out the pond down the hill, backed by Rich Mountain. The pond had almost dried up from the summer's drought. It shone dully, like scattered silver coins of several sizes tossed into tall grass. She'd spent a lot of time there as a girl, look-ing at her reflection. The old-time Harmons used to say that if a young girl looked into a pond, she'd see the man she would marry.

That had never happened, but something strange had. She was seven that summer and had just finished her first year of school. The Harmon family reunions had been held on one weekend every summer, in a field on the other side of the pond, where Granny Maud and Grandpa Henry had once grown corn. She remembered tents set up everywhere, camper trailers. Clouds of barbecue smoke came from under funeral parlor tents. Relatives sat in folding lounge chairs, smoking cigarettes. Lou Ellen played with her cousins by the creek, but whenever she got a chance she slipped off by herself to the pond.

Back then the pond was a pretty place. It was round and silver, like a big dewdrop that had fallen down and flattened out. She stared into the pond, watched the clouds sail by, the surface go dark then light again, watched her reflection. It was already dark when she heard someone calling her. "Lou Ellen? Where in the world are you?" her mother cried. That early evening the pond was like a circle of black velvet with stars stuck into it like pins. The crickets sang in the warm still night.

At the pond the next day, Lou Ellen made a friend out of her reflection. The two of them wove necklaces out of clover, stained their lips with pokeberries, plucked petals from daisies. He loves me, he loves me not. But that afternoon, when she went back, a steel-edged thundercloud passed over, and the water went dark. She smelled rain moving across dry grass, and a cool wind stirred through the trees, rippling the glassy surface of the pond. When it cleared Lou Ellen saw her face again, her own face, but it was new somehow. When she blinked it stared back at her unblinking. It frowned back at her when she smiled. A dragonfly buzzed past her head, skimmed over the water, and alighted near her reflection. The face rose up out of the pond, made out like it would snatch the dragonfly with its tongue, then looked up at Lou Ellen from under the water, calm, lips curled in a smile, eyes upturned. There came a crack of thunder, and the rain came down, making little pockmarks across the face, then all across the pond. Lou Ellen picked up a rock and dropped it over her reflection, watched it ripple outward and outward, then she turned and ran back to the reunion as hard and fast as she could. She had never gone back to the pond after that. She wouldn't go now, either.

That was a long time ago. Lou Ellen walked a little way up the hill, past the cabin ruins, to the place where Granny Maud's and Grandpa Henry's tombstones stood tall and slantwise in the small family plot. GONE HOME, Grandpa Henry's said. CROSSED OVER, Granny Maud's said. Aunt Cora used to tell how Grandpa wouldn't pass a graveyard without a lucky stone in his pocket, how he would stop the clock when somebody died. When Granny Maud heard somebody had passed away, she would throw a quilt over the mirror of her washstand to keep the dead from peeping out of the mirror from the other side.

Aunt Cora had inherited that washstand and had passed it on to her daughter, but Lou Ellen owned it now. It stood in the small room at the top of the spiral staircase, the room George used as an office. Aunt Cora had been dead for years, but when her daughter had learned Lou Ellen was going to build the log house, she thought Lou Ellen might appreciate a family heirloom that fit the decor. She wasn't sure whether her cousin gave it to her out of heartfelt generosity, or because the close proximity of the log house afforded her a good opportunity to get rid of it. The washstand was a lovely piece, though. It was made of burled walnut, with curls of carved wood breaking like ocean waves around the oval mirror. Lou Ellen hadn't been sure where she wanted to put the piece, but there were places all over the house where it would look nice. She wasn't so sure she wanted to look in that mirror a dozen times a day, though. Until she decided where to put it for good, they had put it in George's office, where Lou Ellen seldom had reason to go.

She was back near the house now, pleasingly exhausted from the hike. The peaked roof of the big log house shot up from the tree line like the prow of the Titanic. The windows at the front of the house stared out like square glass eyes. She went in through the back door, then through the mudroom and into the kitchen. She found the basement door ajar. She and George always kept it locked because he said it would be the main point of entry for a burglar. The house had not been broken into yet, but George always said it was a matter of time.

"George?" she called out. He was not supposed to be there until the next day, but it would be like him to come early, or late. He liked coming and going like a tomcat. Maybe he'd decided to get there early and was down in the basement looking at the humidifier that had stopped working on their last visit.

She opened the door to the basement and stood at the top

of the stairs. The basement gaped below her—three thousand square feet of raw space, with a garage next to it. It was dark except for the dim suggestion of a light in a far corner alcove, a light that might have been left on after their last visit. "George?"

No answer. She locked the basement door. It was a good strong lock. Nobody in the great room, the kitchen. The kitchen counter was bare. George always brought his keys in and left them on the counter. She looked out the window—no car in the drive. If George was driving his Jaguar he would have parked in the garage. She wouldn't go through the basement. No, that she wouldn't do. She made sure the front and back doors were locked. The chimes on the front door dinged like hammers on a dulcimer when she locked it. Chimes on a door kept wayward spirits out of the house, the mountain people used to say. They had said so much Lou Ellen couldn't remember half of it. She stepped from room to room downstairs, looking in closets, shower stalls.

She climbed the spiral staircase to the loft. The door to George's study was half open, and she stepped inside. There was a skylight in the room and it was sunlit most of the day, but now, with the sun setting, the light was the color of oxblood. She looked into the mirror. The mountain people had believed a mirror was a portal into the next world— through it the dead looked back at you. There were so many old beliefs about mirrors, she thought. She shut the door to the office and looked in every room upstairs, checked under the beds.

Now she was satisfied there was no one else in the house. No one could get in, not without a big, noisy effort. Still, sleep was a long time coming. The house, though they had stayed in it off and on since it had been built a few years ago, had never seemed like a home away from home. It still felt strange. No matter how much light the floor-to-ceiling windows let in, the place was still dark, oppressive. A giant hunting lodge. Lou Ellen's dainty white porcelain hand, which had been an exquisite little ornament on her French country dresser back home, looked cheap and tacky sitting on the rustic pine dresser.

She dozed off, only to be awakened by the sound of footsteps. Someone had just left the room. She strained her ears. Nothing. Not a sound. She sat up. Her rings and jewelry were still intact on the fingers of the porcelain hand, but a pair of tan leather pumps lay in front of the chair where she always sat to take her hose on or off, to put on or take off her shoes. The shoes lay askew. One was turned on its side. Its wearer had been in a hurry, or careless or tipsy, and had flipped them off. She picked up one shoe as if it were a fragile relic, as if she were an archaeologist and the shoe a dinosaur bone.

Heels clicked across the wood floor in the great room. A kitchen cabinet closed with a thud, and the refrigerator opened and shut. Lou Ellen slipped on her robe and went into the kitchen. On the counter sat an open bottle of red Burgundy. Next to it sat a wine goblet from the rustic stoneware set she kept for use there at the country house. It had a telltale drop of red at the bottom and lipstick on the rim.

Lou Ellen looked up. A shadow, tall and thin, wound around the spiral staircase fast and smooth like a stripe on a barber's pole, and ran blithely across the loft. The door to the study opened, then shut. From the bottom of the stairway she could see light under the door of the study. She picked up the fireplace poker and crept up the stairs. She opened the door. There was no light on, but the full moon shone down through the skylight, making a shining oval of the washstand mirror. The face of the dead would stare back at you from the Beyond, the old mountain people used to say. Lou Ellen walked in and looked straight in the mirror, but saw only her own face. Just Lou Ellen, her steel-gray hair slightly rumpled from sleep. But there was something else, something else they used to say. What was it?

As if to give an answer to the thought, another face floated like a tethered balloon just over her left shoulder. The other face was identical to her own, right down to the faint scar on her upper lip where she'd had a mole removed. The same face, yet different somehow, livelier about the eyes, watched Lou Ellen over her shoulder.

"Who are you?" Lou Ellen asked.

The other raised her eyebrows and mocked Lou Ellen. "Who are *you*?"

What was it they used to say about seeing your double in the mirror?

The other face, as if to answer the question, spread out in a broad and serpentine smile. *If you see your double in a mirror, they used to say, you know your time has come.*

Lou Ellen raised the poker. The other face twisted into a look of mock terror. Lou Ellen whacked once at the mirror. The glass cracked, and a long jagged line like lightning raced downward, separating the one face that remained in the mirror into two ragged halves. One smiling face, hardened and haughty.

George arrived early the next morning. He stood in the middle of the great room. "Lou Ellen?" he called out. "Lou?"

"Up here." He could see the door to his office was open. He climbed the spiral stairs. He found Lou Ellen bent over with broom and dustpan, sweeping up a fairly large pile of dust, enough to fill a shoe box. He looked at the cracked mirror, the bits of glass in the wastebasket, the poker leaning against the washstand. The oddest thing, though, was the pile of dust.

"Lou, what happened?"

"I don't know," she said. That was a lie; she knew exactly what had happened and why. But she could hardly expect him, of all people, to understand.

He bent down, laid aside the broom and dustpan, lifted her up, and took her by the shoulders. He looked at her as if he didn't know her at all. He looked at the mirror, then back at her. "Lou, did you do this?" She gave him a hard look but no answer. He put his arm around her, as he would someone who was very ill and might collapse at any time. "Let's go downstairs and make some coffee, alright?"

In the kitchen, he made the coffee for a change, poured hers as well as his, and stirred in her cream and sugar, something he usually did only during one of his rare bouts of guilt. He looked at her, eyes searching. "Look, Lou, honey, can we talk?"

She shrugged and nodded. And she listened. It was no effort whatsoever to listen, because what he said was so amusing. This last business trip had been nothing but a hassle, he said. He was tired of hotels. Anymore he had a problem with his ankles swelling on long flights. And he knew he hadn't always done the right thing by her. He made a brief reference to his "gallantries with women" and promised to make amends.

"You know, Lou," he said. "I've been thinking about retiring early. A year ago I couldn't stay here in the mountains for a week without getting bored out of my mind, but now I believe I could stay here year-round. I've decided to put the house in Atlanta up for sale," he said. "We can live here full time, you and I."

She shot him a look that poor Lou Ellen couldn't have mustered up if she had tried. His face dropped ever so slightly.

"I don't know about that, George." Lou Ellen had never used that tone with him before.

His face went elastic. "Don't tell me you want to stay in Atlanta," he said. "You've been saying for years how tired you are of the heat, all the people, the traffic."

She looked at him over the rim of her coffee cup. So this was it? For this house, and the others he owned, for this pathetic man with all his virility sapped, his best years spent, for this she had shadowed Lou Ellen off and on over all those years? For this she had visited the scenes of Lou Ellen's life, had shadowed her at playground, school, weddings, funerals, places she worked, sometimes seen, sometimes not? For this she had played peep-eye with her at the pond, had made a little game of toying with her jewels and trinkets, trying on her clothes and shoes, trying on Lou Ellen's life for size? For this she had circled that poor woman like a buzzard circling for carrion, waiting for the right time to swoop down, to take over her dull little life?

Yes, she had. And she'd done it because it is the way of those like her, who choose to step over from the other side, who choose to shadow their others, to covet their lives and sooner or later lay claim to them. She took a sip of coffee and looked out the window. She turned her eyes back to George, shook her head, and sighed.

Now that the game was over, the prize looked cheap. Cheap as a teddy bear won at an arcade. But there was nothing that said she had to take on everything and everyone who'd been in Lou Ellen's life, was there? She'd never liked the man, anyway. Yes, the man would have to go. She crossed her arms and nodded toward the door. "I think you'd better leave, George. And I'm talking for good."

"Lou Ellen, what is it? What in the world is the matter with you?" His lean, taut face had gone to blubber now.

"Nothing is the matter with me," she said.

He looked like he would cry. No wonder—Lou Ellen the Spineless had never once stood up to him. Acquiescence was all she knew. But she felt not a smidgen of pity for him, for either one of them. It was not the nature of her kind to feel much of anything.

"Lou, you're not . . . you're not yourself, somehow," he said.

She laughed at that—a deep, sepulchral laugh that made his eyes widen with terror. Why, she didn't know when she'd ever been more herself. In fact, she felt just like a new woman.

Come, GO HOME With Me

It wasn't the cry of the hawk or the thunder rumbling way off over the ridges that caused him to look up; it was the way it turned quiet all of a sudden. One minute the sourwoods, growing tall behind the yellow-leafed birches, made clouds of red in the river. Then the next minute a cloud passed and blocked the sun, and the river looked like dark glass. Winfred, busy sanding a table under the low-slung tin roof of his porch, looked up at what appeared to him to be a stand of pines— dead, white, stripped of limbs and bark—on the little island in the river. But it was a stand of pines he'd never noticed before, after going on ninety-odd years of looking.

Slowly, features came clear as they would on faces seen through fog. Those were people, not trees, and they stood there straight and somber as a choir, watching him. He half expected them to cut loose singing, but only the hawk, calling out for the second time, broke the quiet. It sailed from the high crag of granite over on High Rock Ridge, cast its shadow across the dark river, and was gone.

Winfred recognized people who'd passed on years and years ago: Uncle Ollis and Aunt Lucille, old Doctor Beal, that sweet-faced Betsy Ames who'd run her daddy's feed store way back in the forties, and the circuit preacher who had come through every year when Winfred was a boy to save, to marry, and to bury. He saw faces of men he'd known when he worked at the lumber mill, and the face of a gypsy peddler he'd seen only once. Faces, not from that bright, sunny place in his memory where people like Hattie dwelled, but from the deep backwoods of his mind, from way back in that dark, piney place where people stayed who had been crowded out by all the faces that filled up his life in later years.

Why was he seeing them now?

Winfred stopped his sanding. Watching them he felt the way he had as a boy when he'd reached the top of Bluff Mountain for the first time and had seen the wide world spread around him, the first time he saw snow hanging heavy on fir trees, or the first time he'd laid eyes on this, his home-place. He felt the way Hattie must have when she saw one of the little people that the Cherokee had talked about. It took him a while to find his voice. "I have to say it sure is a won-drous thing to lay eyes on you all."

"Why don't you come on over then, Winfred?" That was Uncle Ollis talking.

"Come on, Winfred!" said Betsy Ames, sitting down on a fallen log, patting a spot next to her. "It's so nice over here."

"Yeah," said the old doctor, taking the pipe out of his mouth just long enough to speak. "Come on over and visit with us awhile."

The preacher didn't have to open his mouth. The flint in his eyes and the cocksure tilt of his chin said enough.

Winfred narrowed his eyes, studied his company. They sounded just a mite eager, and he had a sneaking suspicion that once he went over there, a little while would stretch a ways into the future. A long, long ways. Still, he held out that they might mean well. "Grateful for the invitation," he said, "But I stick close to home these days."

"Aw, pooh!" barked Aunt Lucille, put out. "Can't be more than twenty feet across!" She'd never forgiven him for not coming to the family reunions over in Yancey County. "Get up off your tail and come over here!"

"Don't think so," Winfred said, hard-eyed. He nodded his head, with full understanding now of what they were up to. "I've got a notion it's a good bit longer from here to there than it looks."

"Stubborn. Still stubborn as a mule!" Lucille said, shaking her head.

"Won't get any argument from me on that point," Winfred replied. "So you all might as well get on with whatever it is you're about. I've got things to do." The next time he looked up they were gone.

The past couple of years he'd thought a lot about all the people who'd gone on before him, which was just about everybody he'd ever known. So he guessed it was not so peculiar that his mind would conjure up people from his past. But why didn't he see somebody he wanted to see? Why didn't he see Hattie? He'd give his last tooth, he'd give up his ninety-two acres here along the French Broad River, to see his child bride just one more time.

Every year about this time, when the leaves came down, the trees went bare, and the frost fell on Winfred's five acres of pumpkins, he wondered where Hattie had gone, what might have become of her. Since she was younger than he was when they married, she might still be living, but then she might just as easily be long gone from the world. He'd never heard from her since she left. After that first long, lonely year, he'd given up trying to find out where she'd gone. He'd finally figured he'd never know one way or another. He'd gone on about his life like he'd done before. He plowed, planted, and reaped. He'd even married Inez, a widow with two boys, but still, in the long years since, Hattie danced like an elf across the green fields of his memory.

Half hoping that when he looked up she might be there where the others had been, Winfred stopped sanding and slowly raised his head. The island was still empty except for the sourwoods and the birches. The sun had come from behind the cloud, and the river was gray again. It was more lonesome now than it had been before all those people came. So he did the same thing he'd done way back when he'd given up on ever knowing what had become of Hattie—he worked like a beaver on the project he found in front of him. He found the stubborn rough spot on the wood and worked harder on it. There was always a spot or two on a piece of wood that didn't want to be sanded smooth, as if the tree, like any man worth his salt, didn't give itself over without a fight.

The visitors he'd had a few minutes ago were right. He was stubborn. And there was a stubborn spot in him that nobody, not even Hattie, had managed to wear down. But there was a reason for that: there had always been something or someone wanting to undo what a man had done. Something was always out to destroy a man's crops, take what he had, or tear down the wall he had built up around himself: trespassers, forest fire, too much rain, not enough rain, acid rain, the blight that destroyed the giant chestnut trees all those years ago, the young man that had taken Hattie from him. And worse, yes, even worse than all that, there was always someone wanting to take the ground right out from under his very feet: the government, developers, logging companies. A man had to stay his ground and watch.

When the government had decided to take over untold acres of mountain land for the Smoky Mountains National Park, his people had been forced out of their homeland near the border between North Carolina and Tennessee. That burned Winfred still. They had come east and settled between the Bald and the Walnut mountains on a tract of land northwest of the French Broad River. Winfred had loved the place as soon as it came into view from around the bend in the wagon road. Here the land rolled just enough to delight the eye, yet still be useful; here the river was truly broad, more so, he had heard, than it was farther south. Wilder, too, in places. "Well, y'all," his daddy had declared when the wagon pulled up, "this here is it."

The first thing his daddy had unloaded from the wagon was his rifle. It was the first thing he took into the house. He parked it inside the front door, and it was understood what it was for: kill a man before you let him take your land. Winfred had run off exploring the new homeplace, had gone a little ways down the riverbank to a place where the river curved around, making a dark and secret little cove. He'd heard Mama calling him, "Winfred, you lazy son of a dog, come back here and help unload the wagon!" But he'd been busy carving his initials on a hickory tree near the water's edge. He swore that day he'd never leave the place alive. Now, some eighty years later, that tree had grown to a giant, been uprooted by floods, been sawed up and burned as firewood, but Winfred was still there.

In all the years that passed he had left home only when he had to: to fight in the war, to work in the CCC Camp, at the lumber mill, or for the railroad. Once he was able to make his living by farming alone, he left only to go to the market in Asheville. He'd socialize a little then. He could talk a blue streak in those days, back when there was somebody of like mind to talk to. And every once in a while, before his hands got stiff with arthritis, he would play the dulcimer and the mandolin wherever players and pickers got together. But all the while he played he itched to get home.

Winfred didn't much care to go anyplace. He didn't even care to hunt over on the other side of the river, over on old man Elmer Langtree's land, even though hunting was good over there. Of an evening he could hear wild turkeys squabbling across the river, could sit on his porch and watch herds of deer drinking at the water's edge. But it wasn't his land so he wanted none of it, and nothing off of it. It was almost an offense to him how steep and rocky it was over there. You couldn't farm it, you couldn't build on it, it was about impossible to harvest trees off of it. It was good for nothing but looking at, which he could do very well without budging from his front porch.

He stopped sanding; the wood was now smooth and ready for the first coat of stain, but it was nearly noon. He'd pick up his brush after dinnertime. He opened the screen door and went inside, shaking his head, thinking about the strange company who'd just come and gone, thinking how he'd lived so long nothing could happen that would surprise him.

He'd already had a big enough surprise that morning when the smell of coffee had awakened him. Still half asleep, in that state of mind where yesterday and thirty years ago and right now get all jumbled together, he'd half wondered if Inez, his second wife, was still with him and had put on the coffee, first thing, like she'd always done. But once fully awake he remembered she'd been dead for years and years. Inez was a practical kind of woman, like Martha in the Bible, who was devoted to him in life, but would think coming back from the grave was just plain stupid, like buying greenhouse tomatoes from the store. On her gravestone he'd had the stonecutter inscribe THE FINEST PEACH IN THE BASKET, and that was the truth, though she'd never had the pull on his heart that Hattie had, and if she had known that, she hadn't let on.

But when he'd entered the kitchen that morning, sitting there at the pine table was, of all people, Jack Dobbins. He was bent over a cup of coffee just like he used to do in the old days after Inez had died, when he'd drop by some mornings on his way home from the late shift at the mill, let himself in if Winfred was still in bed, and put on the coffee. Jack Dobbins hardly ever said a word back then, but tried in his way to keep his old friend company, comfort him in his grief when Inez passed on, just as he'd done years before when Hattie had left and nobody wanted to talk about it.

It was Jack Dobbins sitting there at the kitchen table, no doubt about that. His coal-black hair came down to a point on his low forehead, and he just sat there as if coming up out of the grave were business as usual. He stared into the cup like he was thinking real serious about diving in. Winfred always suspected there was more to his friend than he ever let on, but since he never said much, nobody could ever know what. Winfred, seeing that his friend didn't look or act any different, said, just as he always had, "How're you doin' today, Jack Dobbins?" Nobody had ever called him Jack or Mr. Dobbins, and nobody ever said why.

And Jack Dobbins said, just like he always did, "Can't complain," and he didn't. Didn't say much else either.

When Winfred turned his back to tend to the coffee, which was spewing over onto the stove, he said "What brings you this way, old friend?"

"Just thought I'd stop by," Jack Dobbins said.

"Glad you did," Winfred said, thinking he really was glad. He could do with some company, and if he could get Jack Dobbins to talk a little, he'd try to find out exactly where he'd been all this time and what it was like there, not that knowing any more about it would make him any more eager to go there himself. But just like always it was the two men staring into their cups of coffee, talking about the weather and the old railroad days.

"Well, better get on up the road," Jack Dobbins said after a while, just as he always had.

"Don't be in a hurry," Winfred said, just like he always had. He was standing by the stove pouring another cup of coffee.

"Well, come, go home with me," Jack Dobbins said, just like he used to do. Just about everybody said that back in those days when they were done visiting, and nobody ever meant it. But it was funny how Jack Dobbins said it this time—like he might be earnest about it—and that straightened the curly hairs up and down Winfred's arms.

"Not today, friend," Winfred said, keeping his back turned, "I expect I've got plenty to do around here today."

When Winfred turned around he was by himself again. There was nothing left of Jack Dobbins but the ring on the table that his coffee cup had left there. Nothing remained in the kitchen but Winfred himself and the smell of spilled coffee that had scorched on the burner of the stove.

That had been Winfred's first surprise of the day, seeing old Jack Dobbins sitting at his kitchen table that morning. Now, after the people on the island in the river had showed up, he hoped it would be his last. He stirred the beans cooking on the stove and served himself a bowlful, then went out onto the front porch. Nothing in the world like good eats to bring a man down to earth, he thought.

His company had gone on back to wherever they had come from, but now the Myers boy knelt at the water's edge on the island, dropping in rocks and watching the ripples they made. Sweet-faced and solemn as a calf, he looked up at Winfred. Winfred felt a surge of grief under his heart remembering the day, some forty years ago, when the boy drowned upriver, after a storm. Louis Gosnell had come up out of the river carrying the lily-white body of the boy he'd found caught in a tree fifteen feet above the normal level of the river. The poor boy's eyes were glazed over with fear.

He didn't look a bit afraid now, though. "Come on over, Mr. Brumley," he said.

Winfred sat down in a rocker and ate a spoonful of beans. "Can't now," he said, after the first bite. "It's dinnertime."

"Look what I found," the boy said, holding out his hand as if Winfred could see from that distance, "a gold topaz and a moonstone."

"How about that," Winfred said. "You always were one to find a treasure."

"I can show you where to find gold coins dropped by cattle drovers," the boy said, as if Winfred were a boy and that would entice him to come over.

"Aw now, boy, you go on and have your fun. Ain't nothing over there that interests me."

"Sure there is. There's Indian mounds and arrowheads and a cave with a bear skeleton."

Winfred shook his head. "I'm too old and stiff to swim, anyhow."

"River ain't no more than waist deep right there," the boy said.

Winfred just smiled at him and looked upriver to Spring Creek Mountain where Hattie had liked to climb. The poplars and maples halfway up had already lost their leaves. When he looked straight across the river again the boy was gone.

It left a hole in his heart that hadn't been there before. He wished he wouldn't see anybody else, unless it was Hattie. He guessed it wasn't so peculiar that Hattie's face had faded from his memory after more than fifty years, but it was funny that he remembered her hands and feet so well. He recalled how her sun-browned toes clutched the rocks as she danced over Pawpaw Creek, how her small hand had opened up to show him a fairy cross she'd found in a clearing somewhere on the other side of the river. What had Hattie looked like exactly? Part Cherokee, wide face, big grin, big swimmy eyes. He used to tease her about being one of those moon-eyed people who lived in caves, the ones the Cherokees used to tell about.

Hattie was just fifteen, still a girl by today's thinking, when he took her as his wife. But that wasn't unusual back then, and she didn't have any people, and he, over thirty, had no wife and no prospect of one. Hattie had come up to him at the barn one day, barefoot and brown-eyed. She never said where she came from, so he figured she was the kind of mountain girl who was left alone after her mother died and her shiftless daddy had run off. He gave her food, and she fed the chickens, gathered eggs. He let her stay in the barn for a while, then decided barns were for cows, not young girls. He thought she ought to stay in the house, and for that to look right he knew he ought to marry her. So he did, even though his mama, who was living with his sister and her children up in Sandy Mush, had pitched a fit about it.

He made Hattie go to school, because he had big dreams for her. He thought she might be a schoolteacher or something, so he stayed on her about studying her books and doing her lessons. He let her stay after school to get special tutoring from the teacher, who said she was smart. But he never expected much of her in the way of keeping up a household, so she never learned. Winfred didn't care. He allowed her to stay a child when other girls her age could grow a garden, cook, preserve, clean, and sew as good as any grown woman. He figured she'd pick it up in her own good time.

"That is not a good thing, Winfred," his mama had warned him when she came to visit him, as she did three or four times a year to turn the house upside down and clean it to her satisfaction. "Winfred, what you need is a helpmeet, not a child to raise!" Hattie did help him, he told his mama. "Like how?" she'd asked. Well, when he hurt his back she helped him lace up his boots, he said. His mama had sighed hard at that, had rolled her eyes, had warned him that Hattie acted younger than she really was, but Winfred didn't mind it.

He didn't care that Hattie spent so much time over at Spring Creek Mountain. She loved it over there, where knobs of granite jutted out like the roofs of houses. There was a big thundering waterfall over there that fell away into a creek she called Boogerman Branch, where ferns towered over her when she sat down among them. She liked dredging the creek with her little raccoon hands, digging in the silt for gold, liked coming home and telling him about it. She would beg him to go over there so she could show him. He went one time, but he was too old to play and itched to get back home, back to work. There were fields to plow; there was lumber to cut.

His mama rode him hard about Hattie. He'd pay for letting her wander off like a wildcat, stirring up her wild blood, she said. He didn't own her, he reminded his mama. She would take up with somebody and take off, his mama warned. And sure enough, she started staying after school more and more, and for longer at a time, and was less and less inclined to look Winfred in the eye. Before the last of the leaves fell that fall, before he'd known Hattie a full year, she and the school-teacher were gone. There was still a dull ache in his heart years later.

Thinking of all that, he wasn't able to finish his dinner. He put down the bowl and spoon and looked across the river at the island. He hoped nobody else would show up. It only made him dig up things best left buried. He decided he might as well get started staining the table. He walked over to the shed. He found his way to the back of his workshop, past high shelves full of tobacco tins and cigar boxes filled with every kind of screw and nut and bolt imaginable, and lost himself in looking for a can of walnut stain.

There was whitewash and enamel and turpentine and polyurethane, all in half-empty, rusting cans, some with lids bulging open. He'd loved this place as a boy. Being there was like being lost in a cornfield. No one knew you were there, or so he thought.

"Winfred!" a woman hollered. He turned to find Mama standing just outside the door to the shop, in that long dress and apron like she wore when he was no more than a boy. It was so good to see her.

"Mama?" he said. He wanted to run up and hug her neck, but everyone else he'd seen that day hadn't had a thing on their minds but getting him to go somewhere. So, as much as it pained him to do it, he turned slowly back to the shelf of paints and stains, which had never made any demands on him that he could remember.

"Winfred, are you coming or not?"

Back there where the air didn't circulate, the smell of it all just about made him dizzy. He was confused. For a second he felt like a boy of ten again. "Is it dinnertime already?" he asked, rummaging through the rows of cans to the back of the shelf, where, at about that age, he'd once met a copperhead face-to-face.

She sighed hard, the way she'd always done when she was fed up with his dawdling ways. "Come on, Winfred! I'm not going to stand here calling you all day!"

He turned and she was gone, but his daddy stood by the old combine, watching him. "You going to nag at me too?" he asked his daddy.

"There comes a time, Winfred, when a man just has to give up and go," his daddy said, just as he'd said when Winfred had gone off to war. And then he too was gone.

All that afternoon Winfred spread stain on the table. It turned out a rich walnut brown, and he was satisfied that he'd done justice to it, that it would be of some use to somebody, someday.

The sun fell quickly into the high ridges of the Smokies behind his house. The river was dark except for the dull glow from the half moon. He went inside and let the air flow through the screen door. The nights would soon be too cool for that.

He sat down in his chair and kicked off his boots, then picked up the mandolin from where it leaned against the fireplace with his granddaddy's dulcimer. He set it on the shelf of his belly where it used to rest real nice. But he didn't have as much belly as he once had, and his fingers were too stiff to do more than strum a little. He gave up after a bit and put it back.

He had dozed off in his chair when he thought he heard footsteps on the front porch. He looked up through the haze of the screen, but he saw no one, not even the glassy eyes of that old raccoon that he could pretty well count on paying him a porch visit come full dark.

He laid his head back against the chair and dozed off again. Sometime later he heard the rustle of poplar leaves across the porch.

"Winfred," somebody whispered through the screen door.

It was not Mama's voice, not this time, no. Mama could hardly talk without bellowing. Maybelle Chatham, most likely. Maybelle from up at the Fairview church who stopped by every week to bring him a pie or a quart of Brunswick stew, thinking it would shame him into going to church, thinking wrong.

"Just leave it on the stove, Miss Maybelle. I thank you kindly."

His eyelids were heavy, and he didn't try too hard to open them, hoping Miss Maybelle would go on now, but she walked in, stood over him, knelt down, and took his hands.

"You surprise me, Miss Maybelle," Winfred teased. "I never knew you had such notions about me." He opened one eye to get her reaction, but it wasn't Miss Maybelle's face that met his.

"Hattie? Praise be to God." He guessed she was twenty or so years older than when he'd seen her last. Round brown eyes smiled from a face that had seen some hardship. "I've been pining over you these sixty years. It sure is good to see you."

"It's good to see you, too, Winfred." She tightened her small hands around his big calloused ones. "How have you been doing?" she said.

"If I was doing any better I'd have to shoot myself," he said.

She smiled.

"I'm a sight older than I was the last time you saw me, all wrinkled and bald." He wished he'd known she was coming so he could have taken a bath and shaved, slicked back what hair he had left. "Feels like a hundred years have passed," he said.

"Seems like. Tell me how you've been."

"Well," he said, raising himself up in the chair. "I don't hardly know where to start. I've got by pretty well over the years. Survived, I guess."

A look of regret passed over her face, and then she smiled. "I'm glad to hear it."

"Reckon you'll be wanting me to come along, now?" he asked.

She nodded.

He leaned forward in his chair and started putting on his boots. "Now you know I'd go to the ends of the earth for you Hattie, but. . . ."

She knelt on the floor, helped him work the boots around his feet, laced them up for him. "But . . . what?"

"But I don't see any need to head out right now. Is there a reason to be in such an all-fired hurry? Can't we wait and get reacquainted first?"

She tied his boots. "I don't see why you'd want to wait."

"You know how it is. I've got winter squash and pumpkins to pull. Got a good crop of pie pumpkins this year. Then there's firewood to cut, a lot to do to get a place ready for winter."

She covered his hands with hers and laid her chin on top of them, then looked up at him, eyes shining. "Winfred, do you remember that day a long time ago when you went with me across the river up Spring Creek Mountain, just that one time?"

"It'd be mighty hard to forget it."

"Remember that waterfall, how we walked right up to it and got soaking wet and you said you reckoned that would have to pass for your baptism?"

"Leave it to you to remember such as that!" He laughed, and so did she.

"And remember that little cove at the edge of Panther Creek where moss was green on the big rocks with the creek rushing over it? And how little bits of pure gold got caught in the crevices between the rocks? And how up the hill from the creek those flame azaleas were all blooming, looked like they were on fire, sure as the world?"

"Those were some sights, I'll allow," he said, remembering that place like it was yesterday, really seeing it now for the first time.

"You said then there couldn't be any place anywhere in the world to compare with that spot, except for your own home-place here."

"I did say that. I did for a fact."

"Well, there's places way the other side of the river you've not seen yet."

He didn't say anything for a while. "You'll stay here won't you, Hattie, while I work my way up to going?"

She eased up, patted his hands. "I have to go, Winfred." Hattie looked serious, wise and distant. The little girl had long gone away. "I can't stay here waiting for you to make up your mind."

"But—"

She took his hands and helped him up. "And you can't stay, either. You wouldn't want to, Winfred, if you had any idea. . . ."

He looked ahead through the screen door at the broad river. It was white now with the glow of the moon. They stepped out onto the porch, went down the steps, and walked across the yard toward the river. They both looked back at the old house, with its tin roof and the porch and the table he'd finished and the fields of pumpkins under the moonlight and all the trees over all the fields and the rolling hills he'd called his own for most of his long life. "Say you got something to show me that'll top that?"

"Winfred, I could talk and talk all night and I couldn't tell you what it's like. But just hold on to my arm and keep putting one foot in front of the other. You'll see for yourself, directly."

SOMETHING
Green That Grows

I dread graveyard workday, but I go on anyway. Every year when fall comes around I think to myself: Now, Mattie, just stay home this time and tend to your own business. The sun comes up over the mountain every morning without your meddling; the creek runs on to the river, and the river to the sea. But then, sure as the sourwoods get red along the edges, sure as the apples hang heavy on the trees and there's the smell of burning leaves on the air, I know what's coming. I start laying out my garden gloves, scrub brush, bucket, and spade, and I fix my mind on what I know I've got to do.

There's this graveyard not far from my place, on a green hill that rises above the valley between the Roaring Fork and the Little Pigeon rivers. It lies under the shadow of Mount Le Conte, right here in the Smoky Mountains of Tennessee. On clear days, after a long rain, I can just about see the hill from here.

Time was the graves were mounded and left bare, but here lately we've let the whole place grass over. The way light and shadow falls across it, it looks like a swatch of green velvet cloth rubbed every which way. There are nights when some few of the gravestones give back the moonlight, but more than half the time, day and night, the whole hill is circled in an arm of fog. And that's just as well, because it would not do for my eyes to look on it hour after hour.

My very own people are buried there; their graves need tending to every bit as much as all the others, but come workday I trudge right on by them, right on by Mama and Papa and my two brothers. On up toward the top of the hill I go, to tend the spot where my sister's husband's people are buried.

I've staked out that spot and everybody knows it, though they don't know why and know better than to ask. I like to tend to that place myself, in my own way. I don't want anybody else up there on that day, and I've got my reasons.

We've always had our workday later than most—round about the end of October when the trees have gone bare. A fair number of families around here do their burying there; quite a few show up to work. We clear away limbs and leaves and the wind-blown debris of the past year; we mow and trim and take up old pots of flowers. From veterans' graves we take up little flags, the stars and stripes tattered and faded with time and the weather. We scrub the mold and mildew off the stones, set aright the ones that have lately sunk into the ground, and put out new flags and flowers, sometimes toys at the graves of children. It's hard, hard work, but when it's done it's a sight to behold. I like to stand back and look at it, like to picture how it will look at first snowfall. I feel all different from how I do after a regular working, though it's hard to attach words to the notion. I know I've spent time near the Borderland; I know I've been walking sacred ground.

Then there's the dinner on the grounds, and after that some start up the singing. It's not a rousing, foot-stomping singing; everybody's too worn out for that. My old cousin, Garvin, just lines out a few of the old familiars, and those who care to will join in. "When we've been there ten thousand years. . . ," he calls out, and we sing that line back after him, then wait for him to call out "bright shining as the sun," then we sing that line. It goes on like that to the end, as if we had to be told the words, as if every one of us didn't know those words better than we knew our own names. But that's the way we did way back in the old time, when some couldn't read the words in the hymn-book. We like to remember the old way every now and then.

'Long about dusk there's a general gathering up of tools, dishes, young'uns. "The day is past and gone; the evening shades appear. . . ," Garvin sings out, and we sing it after him, right about the time the harvest moon comes up over the mountain.

Now, I'll go and I'll do my part. I'll clean and scrub the

stones and clear the best I can. I've never been one to mind dirtying my hands. But I won't put out those pots of flowers that my neighbors and women kin put together. Mums that'll dry up in no time, or plastic carnations. Paper flowers dipped in paraffin wax—now, you know that won't last long. I let my women kin fuss over their dime-store decorations, and watch them lay out the food all pretty. I try not to begrudge doing the grunt work for them and me both, just like I always have.

Truth be told, their pretty ways got them further than my smart ways got me. All of them married and, except for Eula, married well enough. It's a sad thing that, in my time, if and how well a woman married was a measure of her worth. By that measure I lost out. I always had rough hands from hard work, my hair pulled back out of my face, which looked hard and drawn by the time I was thirty. I guess that's half the reason I never married, men being the way they are, more eyes— and more you know what—than brains. I did have a chance with Jubal Tucker, but the Tuckers are just different from the rest of us, and that's a fact. Nobody'll go right out and say that except me, but it's the truth. Oil and water don't mix. Neither do the Caldwells and the Tuckers, and neither do the quick and the dead.

It became my little claim to fame, I guess you'd say, that everybody knew they could always count on me to speak the truth and do the right thing whether it was pleasant or not, whether I got credit or not. That's why, out of all my sisters and cousins who'd raised children and grandchildren, my sister Eula chose me, who'd never had any children at all, to look after her boy, Louis, if she were to die before he was grown. I didn't have much of a way with children. Never was one for playing pattycake and whatnot. By the time Louis came along, I was already too old and bitter to see the world with a child's eyes. But I could tend to him well enough, and he didn't grow up a mama's boy, I'll tell you that.

Now, I have to tell you about Louis, or else you won't understand why I feel the way I do about graveyard workday. He didn't grow up to be a whimpering fool. He liked hard work and didn't stand for sitting around chewing the fat. I like to think he picked that up from me. He wasn't one to waste words. There was something about him, though. Something sad, lost, as if home was somewhere else over the far ridges, but he didn't know how, or have the nerve, to start out in that direction. He might have got that from me too, but I made peace with it and went on about my business.

Now, he wasn't game for just anything. He wouldn't have been a deacon if they tied him up and forced it on him, and he wouldn't pray a word out loud in a crowd if it would save his soul and the souls of the whole world besides. But he helped the men add the kitchen and dining hall onto Piney Grove Church, and, with no help at all, he laid the rock for the retaining wall at the back of the old chapel, where the land drops off into the gorge.

And graveyard workday, he'd never miss that, never did until he went off to the war. Why, he would clear and mow and trim and straighten up the whole place by himself if we would let him. And he wouldn't miss the dinner on the grounds that came afterwards, not for all the world.

So, knowing that Louis will be there and Leela, his old love, will likely be there, too, knowing it'll be up to me to stave off trouble, I go. I put on my muddy garden boots and the dress I wear for cleaning. I pass by the mirror; an old woman who looks like a plow horse peers back at me, and I smile at her. She's an old friend, the truest I've found yet. I pack up a rake, hedge clippers, a hoe, and sturdy gloves. And I stash a little American flag in my pocket.

There's already a nip in the air, and it's so clear you can see bald spots where new houses are being built down in Glades and Shady Grove. The trees and the grass are tinged with yellow, everybody's apples are coming in, and baskets of them are a pretty sight at the roadside stands on the way up the mountain. I get there on the early side, before too many relatives arrive wanting to talk. The men put up picnic tables in the grassy field at the bottom of the hill. The women cover the tables with bedsheets. They save old linens just for that. I see a cousin of mine who comes all the way from Mississippi, and some others I haven't seen in a while, as well as the usu-

als. I just throw up my hand at them. I'll speak to them at dinnertime. They're not offended. They know it's my way. It'll
be a big time when the cleanup is over and done with and all
the graves are decorated. But I can't hardly look forward to
it, knowing what's coming.

Here comes my cousin, Garvin. He's the director of this
operation, or believes he is. I know what he's thinking. He's
wondering why I don't work on the graves of Mama and
Papa, which are a far sight easier to get to, instead of those of
my sister and her husband's family way up on top of the hill.
But he knows better than to ask. He nods toward the big pines
fallen over at the bottom of the graveyard where some of the
McLaughlins are buried, just shakes his head, and says,
"We've got our work cut out for us today, hey, Mattie?" That's
his way of asking, "How're you doing?"

"Yeah," I say. "Sooner we get started, sooner we get it over
with." That's my way of saying, "I'm doing alright, and you?"

As I start up the hill, Garvin, just like he did last year, says,
"Now, Mattie, why don't you let one of the young'uns take
that section up there? No use in you climbing that hill," he
says. "Not that you're not able," he adds right quick.

I stab him with my eyes, but I don't say a word. He knows
I've been partial to that part of the graveyard for many years.
Let him think he knows the reason. Let him think the reason
I always want to work that section up there is that Eula's
husband's family moved away and never comes to tend the
graves, and since Eula was my sister and two of her children
are buried there I take a special interest in it. Let him think
that I don't want anybody up there helping me because I'm a
stubborn, crotchety old woman who needs to prove to him
and everybody she doesn't need any help.

So I head up to the top of the hill, dragging my bucket,
rake, and hoe, passing right by the graves of my own family,
which I always plan to tend to after I'm through up at the top
of the hill, although I know somebody else'll get to them. I'll
come back later in the week and take up the plastic flowers
that some of the girls will put on those graves today. I'll plant
a little sprig of something there, something green that grows,

and come back every now and then to see how it's coming along.

Halfway up I stop to get my breath, and I look back down. People have arrived and are setting out pots of mums and daisies from the trunks of their cars. Somebody starts up a chainsaw. They like to get the noisy work over with quick. A mower starts to hum and the smell of fresh-cut grass blows up to me from below.

My heart sinks a little when I see Leela walking up from her car, hauling two picnic baskets of food. Louis sure was a fool over that Leela. She must be in her sixties now. She's got that graying hair in corkscrew curls tight about her head. Her first husband died, and she's married again. I see her new husband standing out from everybody else with his dark skin and high cheekbones that show he's part Cherokee. He's the one who's cutting into that fallen pine with the chainsaw; he's a good twenty years younger than Leela and there's been some talk about it. And there's Leela's granddaughter getting out of the car. Her long hair is the color of a chestnut and hangs loose way down her back, like Leela's did when she was that age. I can tell it's her even with my weak eyes, even at this distance. Law, she looks like Leela did at that age! Neither Leela nor her granddaughter, nor any of them, ever come up to the top of the hill, not on graveyard workday anyway, and I'm glad of it. I don't know what I'd do if any of them were to start climbing up this way right now. Or if Louis shows up and is of a mind to go down and mix with them.

Now it's peculiar how it is near the top of the graveyard. I come to a place that, from the bottom, looks like the top of the hill, but once I get there I see how it flattens out some and goes on up a little way after that. Hunks of granite stick up out of the ground, too rocky up there to dig for burial. Beyond that there's a steep rise and a grove of hemlocks standing tall together like a choir. It's dark underside of those trees; looks like a passing-over place. I don't go there. It's not my time. I turn around and I can't see a thing down below, can't see my neighbors and my kin. Can't see a thing from down that way but the treetops. Beyond in the distance, I see the smoke-blue peaks at the back of a wide rolling stretch of green.

My heart beats hard from the climb. I lay down my tools, drop my behind on a little ledge of granite, and wipe the sweat off my brow. In a shady corner on up the hill a few steps are the graves of my sister Eula, her husband, and their children. I can just make out the little stones covered by running cedar. I look away. I don't go there yet.

It is cooler up here on this northern slope than down below. And breezier. The undersides of the maples flash silver and the hemlock branches wave, make a sound like wind through feathers. A chill comes over me, in part from the cool wind, but that's not all, no, not all. Up here the firs have dropped their nettles for years, have made a thick, soft blanket over the graves that would quiet any footfall. I want to look over my shoulder, but I don't.

I see some fallen limbs, nothing too big for me to lift, so I get to it. I bend over and pick up the little pile. I stand up, my arms full of twigs scratching at my face, my head so light I'm not easy on my feet, when, through the sweat washed down over my eyes, I see Louis walking down the hill. That's my sister Eula's son, Louis. I raised him up from a boy.

There's a little tingling at the back of my neck, but my heart feels heavy. He's tall and blond-headed like his daddy was, has that square jaw from my side of the family. Dressed for hard work like always. Smell of sweet mountain woodruff in the air around him. He stays back a little, never was one to stand in your face. A fir tree is between us; heavy branches shadow his face. He rakes his hand through his hair. "Hey there, Aunt Mattie," he says, soft, shy-like.

And I say, "Good to see you, Louis," and it *is* good to see him. Always is, every time. I wish I could tell what it's like, how there's this rising up in me, same as I imagine there will be on that Great Day in the Morning, when everyone buried here, feet planted toward the east, will rise up to meet the sun. But it's not right, him being here; I don't care what. So I set my mind on what I know I've got to do.

He spots the load I have in my arms and says "Here, let me take that." I tell him no, I've got to be good for something, and start to carry it on over to the edge of the woods and toss it down. He smiles and puts his hand over his eyes to block out the sun while he sizes up what needs to be done. Then he starts dragging the big tree limbs way into the woods, clearing a path for himself as he goes. We don't talk at all, just go about our business, as if it hadn't been a full year since we'd seen each other last. Louis does most of the work. He rakes up every last twig, straightens out his great-granddaddy's grave-stone, which was half sunk into the ground. I lose track of time, but it can't be long until we have that place looking so neat I know if they were to come up here, Garvin and the others would wonder how in the world I did it all by myself.

Louis rubs his hand on his trousers and looks over all the work he's done.

"It sure was good of you to help me out, Louis," I tell him. "You always were so good to help out." *But you ought not to come here*, I need to say, but can't make myself.

"Always glad to lend a hand," he says. And then comes the time I dread. He walks down the hill a few yards and looks toward the bottom, thinking that he'll go and help out down there, too. He sees all the commotion as everybody starts to make ready for the big picnic. I come down the hill a ways and stand behind him.

From the backs of flatbed trucks and the trunks of cars they bring out coolers with jugs of tea and baskets of chicken and ham and whatnot. A few men are still raking and hauling away brush, but most of them are bringing fold-up chairs out of their cars. Ruth Templeton directs the Tilley girls as they spread out the food, and everybody gets ready for the big reward for all of their work. I let Louis look; I don't have the heart to stop him.

"Look, Aunt Mattie," he says. His forehead wrinkles up; he's confused. "Is that Leela?" Now, I know it's not Leela he's looking at but her granddaughter. I don't answer. How would I tell him that the girl he sees is not the girl he loved so long ago? Leela is there, though. Leela, who waited more years than anyone would expect before she married. She waited long after we all knew he wasn't coming back from the war.

His Leela stands not ten feet away from the girl he thinks is her, but he wouldn't recognize the much older woman who is bustling around getting everybody together so my cousin Garvin can say the blessing.

A light passes over his face. When he starts to go down and join them my heart wrenches. I've got to say something. "You know you can't go down there, Louis." I say. I say it with the deep voice, almost like a man's, that I save for when I really mean business. And I do mean business. He can't be one of them, one of us. He stops, but after a minute, seeing that it doesn't quite sink in, I say a little softer, "You have to think of them, son." After a minute he understands and nods his head.

He keeps looking for a while, though, keeps watching them gather around the tables and pass plates and food. Garvin cuts into a big watermelon. Leela grabs someone's child and wipes his mouth with a cloth. I'm so thankful Louis doesn't ask me all about Leela and who she married and all that. I wonder how much he can piece together in his mind after all these years. A little breeze comes up and I smell sweet woodruff again. I was the last one to toss a handful of it over him in his coffin all those years ago.

"Well, I guess I'll go on now, Aunt Mattie," he says after a while. "Reckon I'll see you later."

"More likely sooner than later," I say, and I feel in my bones it's the truth. He smiles. He understands what I mean. He goes on up toward the hill and I have to shut my eyes. When I open them again he's gone.

I make my way a little farther up the hill to the graves shaded by the hemlocks. I bend over his grave and I take up the flag, its stars and stripes washed almost white in a year's time. I put another one down, the way we always do on grave-yard workday for the ones who died in a war. I pull up some of the running cedar that has almost covered Louis's grave and the grave of my sister's only other child, a baby girl who died at birth. When I pull it up it fills the air with the scent of pine and roots grown deep, and I think the whole earth must have smelled just like this at the beginning of time. It's a right pretty vine, long branches with new green blades like crows' feet, looks like it belongs here in this wild place. But you have to keep it back. You have to keep things in their rightful place. I don't like pulling it up, showing the ugly brown underneath, but it needs to be done, and when a hard thing needs to be done, seems like I've always been the one who has to do it. But even I can't pull it all up. I just have to leave some of it like it is. I like a little something green that grows.

At the CLOTHESLINE

Her twenty-seven-year-old daughter, Annie, was all she had in the world, and Nell had always felt like she had her on borrowed time. So for better or for worse Nell usually let her have her way. Nell was glad to have Annie living with her so they could share expenses, even though they looked at things so differently. Nell had come up chopping wood, drawing water from the well, and putting food by for winter, so watching Annie waste half a day out in the sunroom twisting her body into Yoga positions was painful in more ways than one. One day she went out to the sunroom to wash the windows, and there was Annie on the floor, her back bent like a bow, her head looking up toward the sky, her face lit up from the inside. "What's that you're doing?" Nell asked her.

"This one's called 'Salutation to the Sun,'" Annie said. This was back in the 1960s, when all the young people were doing things Nell thought were nonsense. She wanted to shake her head at the foolishness of it, but she didn't because of the fear that Annie might catch her out of the corner of her eye.

When Annie took a notion to cross the Atlantic by freighter to "find herself," Nell didn't understand, but didn't say anything about it. When Annie wanted to climb a Himalayan mountain to search for the mythical snow leopard, Nell dug into her savings to help pay her way. Nell had hoped that if she let Annie follow every rainbow, then maybe she wouldn't grow up thinking something was missing, the way so many adopted children do. Maybe she wouldn't get too curious about her birth mother, that ghost of a woman who still haunted Nell's thoughts after all those years.

Early on Nell had done what she could to dampen Annie's

curiosity before it had a chance to flair up. She'd told her as much of the truth as she could. She'd told her that her birth mother's name was Ina, that she had been one of the young homeless girls who rode the rails back at the tail end of the Great Depression. Ina was too young when she had Annie, too young for the responsibility. So she had left her with Nell, knowing she would take good care of her. Nell had told Annie that she had heard years ago that Ina was dead. Annie had not questioned her much about it, and for that Nell was profoundly grateful.

She was still afraid, though. Over the years she'd talked with other parents who had adopted children, and they'd talked about how the birth parent, mother or father, alive or dead, could grow into a legend in the adopted child's imagination. Birth parents were unknown, mysterious, and could be attractive for that reason. So Nell was always afraid that, even though Ina had been moldering in the ground more than twenty-five years, Annie might one day get curious about her. Ina, no more than bone and hair, still might have the power to twist and twine herself around Annie's mind. Blood was thicker than water.

Nell liked to think Annie had not questioned her about Ina any more than she had because she respected the way she'd been raised. And except for Nell's support whenever she was going through another one of her phases, Annie had never asked her mother for much. But now she was asking Nell the impossible. Annie, who taught fourth grade at the school where they lived near Galax, Virginia, had the summers off and liked to spend that time taking vacations that either "nourished the soul" or "expanded the consciousness." The summer of '61 she'd taken Nell with her to the Georgia sea islands to explore the Gullah culture. The summer of '62 they'd volunteered at a homeless shelter. Now Annie was in a "back to the land" phase and had been talking about the two of them spending the summer at Nell's old homeplace outside of Fancy Gap. The last tenant had moved out and Nell had put the place up for sale, but Annie had the idea that they could postpone the sale, at least for a while. She wanted to go there and breathe fresh mountain air, be one with nature. She wanted the visceral pleasure, she said, of starting and finishing what many people now thought of as menial tasks. But Nell didn't like the idea. For the first time in Annie's life Nell had turned a deaf ear, and had even refused to discuss it.

So Annie had to resort to a little bit of manipulation. It was Nell's sixty-third birthday. It was 1967, and Annie, flower child in bell-bottom blue jeans and gauzy white blouse, sat down on the floor of the screened porch. They'd just shared some iced tea Annie had made from rose hips, and a birthday cake she'd made with whole wheat flour, wheat germ, and honey. The combination of those flavors had nearly made Nell gag, but when Annie had asked how she liked it, Nell had smiled and said, "Well, it was different."

Annie sat down right at Nell's feet, her mole-brown hair falling in a wide fan down her back. Nell laid her hand on Annie's head and fingered the sprigs of dark pink clover woven into her hair. Nell wished she wouldn't do that with the flowers. It sent her mind spiraling back to that awful day in the summer of '42, when they still lived at the old homeplace and Annie, not yet two years old, had nearly drowned in the pond, and bits of pink pond lilies and grass had caught in her hair.

Annie had a present for Nell, something fairly big and flat, wrapped up loosely in white paper. Nell knew before she unwrapped it that it was something Annie had made for her. Annie liked to give what she called "soulful" presents—sand dollars she found on the beach, handmade notepaper, arrangements of clover and wildflowers she'd gathered in a field. This time the present was a framed enlargement of a photograph Annie had taken. Lately, Annie had been into driving around the countryside taking pictures of barn doors, church steeples, old rusty plows, clotheslines. What she saw in a clothesline Nell could not understand. She did like Annie's pictures of little children's clothes hanging on the lines. The little tee shirts and dresses, colorful as Lifesavers, seemed to be swinging and dancing on the lines. Those made her smile. But what was the attraction of women's camisoles, men's long johns, of bed sheets flopping in the wind? "There's something almost mystical about laundry hanging on lines," Annie had said. "Umhum," Nell had said, and let it go at that.

But this birthday picture struck way too close to home. It was one Annie had taken of the old homeplace. Naturally Annie would think her mother had good memories of it, and would therefore think stirring up her nostalgia about the place would make her want to go back there. "Now, isn't that something," Nell said when she looked at the photograph.

The picture, at first glance, was more sky than anything. The lower third of it showed the farmhouse where Nell had lived a goodly portion of her life and Annie had lived the first two years of hers. It was a good picture of the house. It showed the low-slung tin roof, the squatty front-porch pillars, the broad shady porch. The rest of the picture, the biggest part of it, showed the hill behind the house. Nell always thought that hill looked the way a woman's breast does when she is lying down, broader than it is high, slightly flattened. A really bad mudslide would cover the house up so deep there would be nothing left to show that people had ever lived there. The hill rose up higher than the roofline of the house, and at the top of it one lonely old hickory tree still stood, although the tree was now covered over by kudzu. A narrow footpath snaked through tawny heath grass between the top and the base of the hill. The clothesline was about halfway up the hill. The posts of the clothesline tilted in toward each other, and the sagging lines gleamed like nickel against a coal-black sky.

Nell had planted kudzu to keep the hill from washing away. Now it had covered up the patch of garden where she used to plant sunflowers and zinnias, had crept down and started in on the clothesline itself, the way kudzu will do. You had to burn that stuff back every year or it would take over the whole hill and cover up the only good space they had for the vegetable garden. Harve Brewster, who had been Nell's last tenant and had just recently died, had let it go for a while. Now vines with leaves as big as hands snaked around one post, and minty green fingers of new growth had started curling across the lines. The scene in the picture was heavy with gloom. The air was charged. It was fixing to storm.

"My word," Nell said. She felt dread fall like a slow drizzle over her. Annie misinterpreted Nell's mood as awe, nostalgia.

"It's still a beautiful old place, Mama," Annie said. And that it was. Though the house was small and worn like an old shoe, it sat well against the slope of the hill, with the smoke-blue Pinnacles of Dan away to the east. When Nell had lived there the place had nineteen acres of pasture and field corn and a small orchard near the house. Another house, not in the picture, had been on the property, too. It was not much more than a shack now. It stood farther down the hill, near the pond. That was where the hired hands usually stayed, and Nell didn't have the best memories of that place. She was glad Annie hadn't taken a picture of that too.

"Do we have to sell it just yet?" Annie asked. Nell felt sick in the pit of her stomach. She said nothing. She stood, gathered up the cake plates, and went into the kitchen. She couldn't tell Annie this, but Harve Brewster's death was like an answer to a prayer. No, she didn't want him to die, but when he did it opened up the door. She wouldn't have sold the house out from under the Brewsters for anything, so when Harve died it was like Providence telling her it was safe to sell it now, to go ahead.

Harve Brewster had lived on the place for twelve years. He died back in April, and Nell had gone up there to make a condolence call on his widow. Before that Nell had gone there only when she felt like she ought to. She'd gone when new plumbing had to be put in or the septic tank flushed out, or after a heavy rain when she wanted to satisfy her mind that the hill above the house hadn't started to wash. When Harve's wife was sick she felt like she ought to do something, so she made a chicken pie and took it to them for their supper. She hadn't wanted to stay long, but that Harve was a talker and was beside himself with worry about Lola and his own health, which had already begun to fail.

It was night by the time she was able to get a word in, say her good-byes, and leave. She had started her car and was backing out of the driveway when the headlights caught

Harve's overalls hanging up there on the hill among other clothes on the line. The overalls had faded to a blue so pale they appeared white. It looked like a man standing up there stock-still in the dark. The dew was falling, and she knew it would be neighborly to go up there and get those clothes in for Harve, but she couldn't bring herself to do it. She couldn't put one foot in front of the other and walk up that hill. She decided right then to sell the place whenever the Brewsters passed on.

It turned out that Lola Brewster held her own, but Harve had died right after Easter. Lola went to a nursing home, and Nell had gone over to the place just long enough to meet the Realtor and put a price on it.

Now Annie wanted to change Nell's well-laid plans. Annie followed Nell into the kitchen. She laid one hand on her mother's shoulder.

"It's time to sell it, Annie," Nell said. She stacked the plates in the sink and ran water over them.

"How come, Mama?"

"The taxes are getting too high," Nell said. "It costs too much to keep it up. Besides, staying there wouldn't be like you think." Even with all of Annie's work at plant nurseries and tree farms and the times she had helped handicapped kids ride horses, she'd never really lived in the country, and Nell reminded her of that. "It wouldn't be all tiptoeing through the meadow picking daisies," Nell said.

"Goodness, Mama! It wouldn't be like the old days, either! We won't have to churn butter and make lye soap, or kill hogs!"

"Maybe not. But it's miles from a store. There's no air conditioning. The power comes and goes. The Brewsters were satisfied cooking on the old woodstove, so I never replaced it with an electric one. That means you'll have to chop wood."

"I'd love to chop wood! To smell fresh-cut wood. To get my hands calloused!"

"There's an old ringer washer, but no clothes dryer."

"Oh, I love the smell of clothes that have hung out on the line!" Annie said.

"The ad the Realtor put in the paper calls it a 'fixer-upper that needs some TLC,'" Nell said. "That means it's a wreck."

"You know I'm handy with a hammer and a paintbrush, Mama. In a few weeks' time we can fix it up, and if you decide to sell it—"

"You can bet I'm going to sell it," Nell said, sealing the plastic lid over the cake plate with more force than she had to. She rarely used that tone of voice with Annie.

Annie was quiet for a moment. "Alright, Mama. When you decide to sell it, we can get more for it. Just for the summer, Mama, please?"

Nell didn't say anything for a while. "Alright," she said after a long sigh. "Just for the summer."

They moved in and started right away cleaning up, fixing up. The kudzu had taken over the big garden space, but they found a little spot not far from the house where Annie made a raised garden big enough for them to plant some tomatoes, some bush beans. Nell paused a minute from washing the windows on the front porch and watched Annie scrape the paint off the pillars. Annie said she was going to paint them "country cream." Nell enjoyed a few minutes of thinking it might be alright for her and Annie to stay there for the summer. Sometimes things turned out not half as bad as you thought they would. Sometimes. Maybe this was the thing that Annie had been looking for all this time, without even knowing it. Maybe they would pass a few pleasant weeks here, and Annie would go on to her next phase. Better yet, maybe this dose of domesticity might make her want to settle down, find a nice man, marry.

She'd been born here, Annie had, right down the hill in that little house, which was not much more than a shack now. She had toddled around and taken her first steps at Nell's feet right up there at the clothesline and at the garden. Ina had played with her some, like a child playing with her babydoll, but it was Nell who had held her when she had the chicken pox, and had wiped her snotty nose. A lot of memories could be stirred up at the clothesline.

But for now Nell took a minute to be proud that she was,

against all odds, still the owner of the place. She had held on to it, and now it was hers to sell. It had been part of old Judd Henry's big farm. Nell's daddy had been one of his tenants, and when Daddy died, Nell, her mama, and her little sister, Hissy, couldn't make enough yield to suit Judd Henry. Every two weeks, it seemed like, Judd Henry would threaten to evict them. That was an awful feeling, never knowing when they'd have to go, knowing they didn't have a place to go. She couldn't stand the fact that Judd Henry had the power of life and death over them. Nell was a worker, not a dreamer, but she had that one dream: to hold on to that place. When Mama died and Hissy married the Syles boy and went off to Richmond, Nell stayed. She hired men to help out whenever she could but did most of the work herself. She squeezed bile out of every dime and managed to hold on to the place and buy it from Judd Henry's estate when he died, but a lot happened before that day came.

It had been hard, backbreaking work. But Annie didn't remember those days. This summer stay at the old homestead was like camping out to her. She'd never had to use an old woodstove like the one in the kitchen, and knew she wouldn't have to forever, so naturally it was fun to her. Annie thought the old rickety ringer washer, with its small tub and three legs, was sweet. She liked the way it danced across the floor when they used it. Annie didn't know what it was like to have to hang clothes on the line because there was no other way to get them dry, so to her hauling a laundry basket full of clothes halfway up the hill and battling the sometimes high winds to get sheets hung was not drudgery, it was an adventure.

The first time Annie hung clothes on the line she told Nell it felt like "a rite of spiritual purification," or some such. Nell just shook her head and warned her that it would get old quick. Annie said she didn't think so. Nell wished Annie wouldn't spend so much time up there. "You'll have enough to do being the woodchopper, the painter, and the carpenter," Nell told her. "You ought to let me be the cook and the laundry woman." So while Annie finished the work on the porch Nell did the cooking. She washed the clothes and hauled them, as she had so many times for so many years, up the slope to the clothesline.

Annie had straightened up the posts as best she could and had pulled the lines taut. She had yanked off the curling fingers of kudzu, but they had left their marks all over the posts. Because of the way the mountains cast shadows, and because the spruce pines made so much shade, and so much of the sunny ground was rocky, there had never been a big space for a clothesline or a garden near the house. A garden or a clothesline shouldn't be where you have to walk uphill to get to it.

Not far from the clothesline lay the wide slab of granite where so many times she'd seen timber rattlers sunning themselves. She was never afraid of timber rattlers; they weren't as territorial as copperheads. But that slab of granite attracted lightning, and she was afraid of lightning, with good reason. Lightning was always striking up there. She remembered how it could come up so quick, with only a few lazy rumbles of thunder. She'd think she had time to run up and get the clothes off the line, then—out of nowhere—FLASH! BOOM!

She was just a girl when that old hickory tree was struck and split down the middle, and had come back alive, or seemed to. Now kudzu hung so heavy over the tree it looked like a giant woman bent over, draped in mourning clothes. Beyond the clothesline, beyond what had been the garden, loomed the western sky, where you could sometimes see storms coming.

Right now, though, the sky was blue. Nell kept her mind on hanging the clothes. Pick up Annie's overalls from the clothes basket, pin them to the line. Press them out with your hands to smooth the wrinkles. That was one way to keep her mind from wandering. Nell finished hanging all their denim and cotton work clothes, their underwear, nightgowns, housecoats. The clothes looked like they belonged there. Before she made it back down the hill it came up a wind. The clothes dried quickly, and she had them down and folded and put away hours before the dew fell.

That night Nell lay in the bed in the room that had been

hers when she was a young girl. It was hot, and she had left the window open. Something woke her. She sat up to hear what it was. It was deathly quiet. It was the quiet that had awakened her. The loud, rhythmic *chee chee chee chee* of the cicadas had died down suddenly. She didn't know why. The moon was over the house somewhere, out of her view, but the light of it shone through the part in the curtains. A little breeze lifted the hem of the curtain and showed the clothesline gleaming silver halfway up the hill. The curtain fell, then stirred again. In that next momentary lilt of the curtain she saw clothes hanging from the line. A string of long white chemises danced in the light wind like fairy girls in long white petticoats. She shut the window, hot as it was, and pinned the curtains so not a sliver of moonlight could get in, and so she could not see out.

She lay there on her side, turned away from the window toward the wall, sweating, thinking. When Nell was a teenage girl she'd written her name over and over right where the bed butted up to the wall. The wall and her name had been whitewashed, but she could still make it out. Eleanor. Nellie. Nell. Good old Nell, that's what everybody called her. Good old Nell, like she was somebody's mule. Oh, how she wished she could forget those days.

It was back in the last years of the Depression. War was coming. Nell was halfway to forty. Already she had nursed all the old people, made the white cake for all the brides. Every time she watched a new bride slip the knife into the virgin white cake, it was like a knife slicing through Nell's own heart. It wasn't a man's love she wanted, or so she had thought, so much as the kind of help a hardworking man could give her, or the son or daughter any kind of man could help her get. A son or daughter who could help her take care of her place, or help her out when she was old.

By the time a man came along she'd buried both parents, and her sister, Hissy, was married and gone. Plant the garden, work the garden, sell what you could, and put the rest up in jars for the winter. Chop wood, draw water. That was her life. Listen to Dinah Shore or "The Guiding Light" on the

radio of an evening. Every day the sun rose and set, and nothing changed but the seasons. Many was the time she'd stood
on that hill, hanging clothes in the early morning, wishing
something, anything, different would come from the other
side of the mountains, like those rays of sunlight peeping
through the gap.

One day a ray of sunlight, or what passed for one in her
beat-down state of mind, came up the hill in the person of
Hal Martin, a hobo who hopped off the train in Galax. He was
heading up the hill toward the house about the same time she
was walking down from the apple orchard. She invited him
right in the house, where he sat at the kitchen table, his hat in
his lap, while she served him biscuits and apple butter. He
said he'd harvested peaches in South Carolina, apples in
North Carolina, and was heading north with the sun and the
harvest. The long and the short of it was that he needed some
work, and she needed a hand. She told him she couldn't pay,
but he could stay in the little house down the hill, where
they'd always let the hands stay, and share what food she had.

Hal Martin stayed for close to a year, and he was good for
everything around the place. And that meant everything,
even that thing which Nell didn't know, until he showed up,
that she needed so bad. It happened everywhere, too—out in
the orchard in summer, on the floor in front of the fireplace in
winter. She didn't care what anybody would have to say
about it if they knew, either. She'd been good all her life and
it had gotten her nowhere. Being bad didn't get her anywhere
either: the main thing she hoped to get out of it was a baby,
and, for some reason, it had never happened. In her private
thoughts she blamed it on Hal.

She could tell Hal got itchy for greener pastures. He heard
there was work building roads in North Carolina with the
Civilian Conservation Corps. He would send the money he
made back to her. When he came back on his first leave they
would get married, he said. She didn't believe he'd be back.

Well, he came back for his first leave, and for his second. On
his third leave he came back dragging a young pregnant girl,
Ina, with him. So there was good old Nell stuck with the two

of them, and that was when the trouble had started. She didn't want to think of all that now. It was all over and done with.

She never knew what had become of Hal, but Ina was up there in the garden that was now covered over by half an acre of kudzu. "You're dead now, Ina," she said, more a statement of hope than belief. "You can't touch us now."

The next day Nell was walking down the hill from the clothesline when she tripped and fell to the ground. She hollered, and Annie, who was up on a ladder painting the siding of the house, dropped her brush, jumped down the ladder, and ran up to her. "What happened, Mama?"

"I just tripped is all," Nell said, but it crossed her mind that she *had been* tripped. There was a lot of difference between the two.

She spent the next two days on the couch the Brewsters had left on the front porch. She sat with her swollen foot propped up on pillows. She snapped beans and mended clothes while Annie painted, mowed, cooked, and hung the laundry on the line. They were doing a lot of washing, all the muslin curtains on all the windows, all the bed linens stored in trunks. So Annie spent a fair amount of time at the clothesline. She was a pretty sight up on the hill, in her bell-bottom blue jeans, with her gauzy blouse and long hair blowing. Every once in a while Annie's humming or singing carried down on the wind. "Are you going to Scarborough Fair?" she'd sing. "Parsley, sage, rosemary, and thyme. . . ." Nell felt useless, but Annie seemed happy, for now anyway. Several days passed like that. Sunny days, calm weather.

But the day came when Annie walked down from the clothesline, the empty basket on her hip, with a funny look on her face. "You know, Mama," she said. "I got the funniest feeling up there on the hill."

Nell jabbed her finger with her sewing needle. "What kind of feeling was that?"

"I don't know. Déjà vu. Like I've been there before." She laughed. "Of course, I guess it stands to reason since I *have been*, or I guess I was, when I was a little girl. But, funny, I'm only just now starting to remember."

"You were barely walking when we left here," Nell said. "I don't see how you could remember much."

Annie sat down on the front-porch steps and picked at her toenail. Nell could see only the back of her head, her hair spread across her back. Annie asked, "Did we have some kind of dog when we lived here?"

"There were several dogs, off and on through the years. Hunting dogs."

"Blue." She turned and looked at Nell. "Was there a dog named Blue?"

"We might've had one named Blue. There were so many of those ole bluetick hounds around. Probably called half of them Blue."

"Blue!" she said, as if she remembered for certain now. "I thought so."

That afternoon, Annie had picked beans and brought a bucket of them to the porch where Nell sat, her foot up, waiting to start snapping them. She sat down next to Nell, looked her square in the face, and asked the question Nell dreaded most. "Mama, what was she like?"

Nell stopped snapping beans, then started up again, looking off toward the mountains. "Young, not much more than a child herself."

"Pretty?"

Nell shrugged. She remembered Ina as all leggy and wilted, like a pansy struggling to survive in the July heat. "Pretty enough," she said. *Enough to get what she was after*, Nell thought, though it probably didn't take much more than being an easy throw-down to get what she wanted. She was already pregnant when Hal brought her there.

Nell would never forget how happy she was to see Hal heading up the hill, until she craned her neck to see who was walking with him, and saw it was a young girl. "What was I supposed to do, Nellie?" Hal had said. "She claims it's mine." He was a pitiful sight, sitting there slumped over, his face in his hands. What a fix for her to be in. She could hardly afford to keep herself up, and now there were two more mouths to feed and a third on the way. Nell was just about to send them both on their way, but then she thought better of it. Judd Henry had been threatening to kick her out. He'd said he needed a man to run the place, make it pay. With Hal there, with a hardworking man around the place, maybe Judd Henry would think again. Her eyes burned, but her voice was steady. "You and that girl can stay down at the little house," she said, "but just till you get on your feet."

Annie was talking again. "But what was she really like?"

"She didn't have a lot of get up and go," Nell told her. "Didn't have much common sense."

She almost laughed at what an understatement that was. That Ina was the sorriest, whiniest, laziest thing. Ina didn't have the sense God gave a dog. Couldn't make a biscuit, didn't know the first thing about planting, picking, pickling, preserving. So Nell planted more and gave them the surplus. Cooked and fed them. She couldn't bear to see Annie, who came in the fall, go hungry.

Ina had a hard time delivering, and Nell helped the midwife bring Annie into the world. Annie was not more than two or three weeks old when Hal banged on Nell's door in the middle of the night, woke her up from a dead sleep, and handed her the baby. Ina had tried to do something awful to the baby, but he wouldn't say what. "I think she's gone crazy, Nellie," he said.

Nell snatched the baby from him and held her so tight to her breast the child started to cry. "I always thought she was crazy," Nell said. "She's not fit for a thing."

Hal got drafted in the fall of '42. Nell couldn't turn out Ina without turning out Annie as well, and she'd become attached to the baby. When Hal wrote home, it was to Ina, not Nell. Ina would come up to the clothesline to read the letters out loud. Nell would act only half interested. She'd hang the clothes at a nice brisk clip, pressing the wrinkles out of each piece as she went along, while little Annie toddled at their feet. The letters were shrunken, not much bigger than the palm of Ina's hand, and she was young enough, foolish enough, to think that was cute.

Ina, if she wasn't good for much else, was good to play

with Annie. And why not? She wasn't much more than a kid herself. She'd sit down with Annie and cut out pictures. She'd set Annie up on Blue, one of those old bluetick hounds that had come down from the pack of hunting dogs Nell's daddy used to have. She'd hold her up and let her ride Blue like a horse. Annie liked to hide behind the sheets that hung low to the ground. Ina would call out, "Where are yoooou?" And Annie, thinking since she couldn't see them, they couldn't see her, would jump out. Ina would holler and they'd break out into giggles. But then Ina would let Annie run loose and eat pokeberries or get eaten up with poison ivy, while she entertained tramps who got off the train at the junction.

"Somebody must've wrote your name on half the boxcars between here and Chicago," Nell told her one time when they were both hanging clothes on the line.

Ina had a collection of those silky camisoles she had ordered from the Sears and Roebuck catalog. She made a big show of hanging them up to dry right next to Nell's old, oversized housecoats.

"I'm glad somebody has got time to care about fool things like that," Nell said.

"The men don't mind it," Ina replied.

"I'm sure your kind would know," Nell shot back. That's how it was whenever she and Ina would meet at the clothesline. They were at each other like two cats.

When Annie was nearly two years old and could run around on her own and get into things, Ina, preoccupied with herself or her men, got more and more careless with her. Then came the day when Annie wandered down to the pond, and Nell just happened, by the grace of God, to be on her way to the garden and heard Annie cry out. She jerked her head in the direction of the cry and saw the toddler, looking no bigger than a duckling, flailing her little arms at the edge of the pond. Nell flew down there, yanked Annie out of the water, and pressed down on her back so hard she knew she might break her bones. She couldn't believe so much water could come out of two little lungs. Nell took Annie home with her. Ina beat on the door half the night, begging, crying out, "Give me my baby! Give me my baby!"

All that next day and night it rained, and by noon the following day weeds had taken over the garden. Nell was hoeing with Annie at her feet when Ina came up the hill carrying a traveling bag and wearing a traveling hat. "I'm going back to my people in West Virginia," she said.

"If you've got people, they probably don't want you," Nell said. "And how do you expect to get there? You going to walk?"

Ina took out a wad of cash, quite a lot of money for that day and time, more than enough for a train ticket, enough for ten train tickets. Enough to buy off old Judd Henry for a few months, too. Nell knew she didn't get that kind of money from the tramps who came by, but lately she'd had quite a few "gentleman callers."

"I've come to get my baby," Ina said as she started toward Annie, who was playing with a corncob doll not far from Nell's feet.

Nell stopped hoeing and wiped the sweat off her brow with the back of her hand. She glared hard at Ina. "You'll leave the baby here with me," she told her. "You're not fit to be a mother."

"I'm her mama!" Ina cried. "And blood's thicker than water!"

By that time Annie had crawled over to the edge of the garden where some morning glories had taken root. She was grabbing at the big purple flowers when a copperhead whipped like a lasso at her head, missing her chin by a hair. Nell ran over with the hoe and with one whack severed the snake behind its head, but she kept on whacking at it and whacking at it. Annie started to cry. Nell's hair came unpinned and sweat flew as she whacked and whacked until that snake lay like ground-up sausage in the weeds. "You're crazy!" Ina screamed. "You're crazy! Give me my baby!"

Ina reached for Annie, and the child, crying and frightened, reached up for her. That went through Nell like a knife. She kneed Ina to the ground, raised the hoe, and sank it into Ina's skull. She stared down at Ina. One blow had not done it. She raised the hoe high and brought it down another time, harder.

Annie screamed raw and ragged. She balled up her tiny hands into fists and beat the air. Nell dropped the hoe and picked her up, held her to her breast, rocked her back and forth, back and forth, to stifle her sobs. "That's a good baby," she said. "That's Nell's baby. That's right. That's Nell's baby."

She carried Annie sobbing, hiccupping, into the house. She rocked her back and forth, bathed the spatters of blood off her, let her play on the floor with Blue. It was dark by the time she got her calmed down. When Annie fell asleep on the floor with Blue, her little arm around his big warm body, Nell shoved her bloodstained housecoat into the woodstove so she could burn it later, and slipped outside to do what she had to.

Outside in the dark she uncurled Ina's white hand, which was not yet stiff, and took the money from it. She went to the shed for a shovel, then dug a grave in the soft wet ground where the sunflowers and zinnias grew. She dug the hole as deep as she could. She dug until she had only enough strength left to drag Ina the few yards to it. She took her foot and shoved Ina in. She dropped Ina's hat in the hole and her bag in with it.

It was getting toward midnight when she smoothed the earth over Ina's grave. Hal had brought back some cuttings of kudzu when he worked at the camp. He'd bragged about how they'd planted it all over the place to stave off erosion, how it grew so quick you better stand out of its way. She'd been suspicious of it and had never planted it, but had kept it in a big iron pot, slinging dishwater over it every once in a while. It had taken over the ground around the pot. She pulled some up and planted it on Ina's grave. In the days that followed she could almost watch it grow and take over.

She wrote to Hal and told him the girl had run off and had left the baby with her. It was easy for him to believe that. By the time he came home from the war, the ground where she'd buried Ina was grown over with kudzu. He hadn't cared that much for Ina, anyway. He was glad to have her out of his hair. She was almost as much a burden to him as she had been to Nell. He didn't feel responsible for Annie either. He didn't stay around long, and when Annie was old enough to notice she didn't have a daddy, Nell told her he'd been killed in the war. For all she knew he had been. She didn't know for sure who Annie's real daddy was.

Nobody came from West Virginia asking about Ina. The gentleman callers came and Judd Henry, naturally, wondered where she had gone, but Nell told them she'd run off somewhere. Times being like they were, and Ina being a road tramp to begin with, they could believe it. Nell decided to keep the place for as long as she could so she would have some say over what was done. She couldn't have anybody burning back that kudzu, digging up that space again for a garden.

Now, twenty-five years later, Nell told herself that it wasn't likely that the old garden would be dug up, whether she kept the house or sold it. She sat on the front porch sewing buttons on one of those flimsy gauze blouses Annie loved to wear. She looked up at the kudzu rising like a dark-green ocean wave above the clothesline, where Annie was taking down some sheets. You could count on few things in this world like you could count on kudzu. Its roots ran deep in the soil; it stayed its ground. She liked to think it had wound itself in and out of Ina's bones by now, pinning her into the earth.

A thunderhead rose like a granite knob above the kudzu-covered hill, and far off the sky rumbled. The clothes—Annie's overalls and tee shirts, Nell's housecoats—flopped in the wind. The sheets and curtains bloused and waved, whiter than white against the black sky. Annie had disappeared somewhere behind the sheets, the way she often did when she was hanging them or getting them in. A little breeze raced down the hill, and Nell spread the collar of her housecoat to feel its coolness. The wind carried Annie's voice down with it, and Nell heard Annie humming to herself, then talking to herself. Then she heard, or thought she heard, two voices talking. She knew the wind could distort sounds. Still, it seemed like two voices spoke in rushed whispers, like two neighbors who had some good new gossip to pass between them.

Nell stood up, held on to the porch post, and strained her eyes to see what she could. She saw the shadows of Annie's long arms as she unpinned one end of a sheet on the line.

Then she saw the shadows of two more arms taking down the other end. Two distinct shadows fell bold and black across the hill. Nell's heart raced. She called out, "Annie? You going to be nightfall getting those clothes in?"

Annie's face peeped out from behind the sheet she was taking down. She clasped it tight against her like Eve hiding her nakedness. She looked down Nell's way, not answering. The other shadow was gone. Nell knew she couldn't trust what her eyes had seen, ought not to trust her mind here lately. On the other side of the clothes that Annie had left hanging, Nell thought she saw long gray rags hanging loose, like lynched men. The thunder rumbled, closer, louder.

"Annie, come down here right this minute! It's fixing to storm! Leave those clothes be!"

"They'll get rained on, Mama!"

"You know that don't matter! Do like I say!"

Annie raised and dropped her arms in frustration. She worked at the clothesline for a minute, then, leaving most of the clothes hanging, the ones Nell could see, she hoisted the basket on her hip and galloped down the hill, the clothes basket bouncing at her side. The look in her eyes gave Nell chills. She looked almost . . . amused. "Mama," Annie said, "look what somebody hung on the line." She pulled from the clothes basket what might have once been a garment, but now to call it a rag would be giving it too much credit. She held it out away from her, gave it a little shake, and it crumbled to the ground like dried bread.

Nell put her hand to her chest, shut her eyes. "I want us to leave here, Annie. We've got to go today."

Annie looked up toward the clothesline. The posts and the line looked pewter against the black sky. It thundered in earnest now. She looked back at her mother. She had a look in her eyes like she was trying to make some kind of choice and was having a hard time of it.

"Annie!"

Annie's eyes cleared. "Alright, Mama," she said finally. She went down on her knees and patted Nell's hand. "Alright."

Nell tried to stand. "I'll start packing up," she said.

"No, you sit back down right there and keep that foot up. I'll do the packing. But first I'll run up and get the clothes in. It's fixing to storm, like you said." Thunder rolled louder now.

"Just leave the clothes be!" Nell said, but Annie had started up the hill. The wind whipped Annie's face, wrapped her hair around her throat. The tall grass on the bald bent flat against the ground. The white sheets and curtains billowed out against that curtain of black. It was so much like the picture Annie had taken. Annie, reaching up to unpin a sheet, was hidden from Nell's view. Nell couldn't see her feet or the top of her head. Sheets and curtains waved and swirled in the wind like magicians' capes, and Annie was lost somewhere behind them. Lightning ripped through the sky like a razor through black cloth. A boom like dynamite shook the porch, bounced off the tin roof of the house. The thunder rolled away like steel kegs. "Annie!" Nell started up the hill, dragging her foot behind her. She pulled herself up, on up, hobbled as fast as she could, though she knew well before she made it up the hill that Annie was not there, and she'd be at a loss to explain to anybody how she knew that Annie was never coming back.

STRANGE
Things Happen

She had started out that day with what she thought of as the August feeling. August has always been the time when back-to-school ads appear in newspapers, new clothes have to be bought, new teachers won over, new friends made, and all the attendant fears faced. August is the time when anticipation is tempered by the passing of the mystic days of another summer.

It was an early August morning. Sam, her only child—her whole world in a four-foot-two, seventy-pound, white-haired package—was eight. The divorce was final, the lawyers paid, goods divided, visitation rights decreed. Her new job, at a bank, started next week. This was home. Charlotte, the New South city. Susan leaned over the kitchen counter in her new apartment and looked across the stacks of unpacked boxes to the soon-to-be-blistering-hot concrete patio outside. No material on earth was as depressing to her as concrete. Unless it was steel. The best antidote: mountain peaks, gorges, falling water. She thought of a favorite place from her childhood. She hustled Sam out of bed, and within the hour they were on their way.

The place was Sliding Rock, deep in the Pisgah Forest. He wanted to know how far away it was. More than a hundred miles, she told him. How long would it take to get there? Three hours. They could go there and back in a day. Are we there yet? He was her only child, the only one she would ever have, and she had never tired of answering his questions or explaining things to him. A river, the Davidson River it is called, winds alongside the byway in the Pisgah Forest. It is more like a wide creek than a river. Clear water sparkles over amber, egg-shaped stones. They stopped and tiptoed across dry rocks to the other side, then back again. Where does the river go from here? To the sea. The creeks work their way to the rivers. The rivers find the sea. The sediment from the erosion of these very mountains had, over thousands of years, made its way into the creeks, into the rivers, and down to the sea. It was in the very sand they'd used to build their sand fort at the beach, back in June. "Cool!" he said.

Sliding Rock had not changed. It was, and is, thick and dark with mountain laurel. Water sheets down sixty feet of gently sloping granite into clear, shallow pools. In the bathhouse they changed into swimsuits. Together they climbed to the top of the rock and careened the long slick way down, plunging into the ice-cold water, bobbing up, gasping, choking, laughing. She'd done that a thousand times before, but this time, with her son, it was new.

Why hadn't she brought him here before? Because she had been depressed off and on for years. She knew he had suffered because of it. Well, no more. Today she was a child herself again. Whee! A few more slides and she pleaded old age, toweled off, and took her place in a folding chair beside the parents, grandparents, and onlookers with cameras. Heat, concrete, steel, sadness—all a world away. She shivered, then wrapped a bath towel around her shoulders. Even the air was green.

From the banter of the parents and grandparents all around, she could soon tell which child belonged to which parent, and which children had come together. Everybody belonged to somebody or had come with somebody. All but one. A boy, maybe a year or so younger and of slighter build than Sam, played alone. He was brown as a hazelnut from the summer sun, built out of wire, with a round head and a grin that opened up his whole face. He seemed to belong to no one. No one met him at the bottom of the slide or hung off the observation deck warning him to be careful. No one cheered him on from the sidelines. No one stood by taking pictures, not of this one.

He didn't seem to mind though. He didn't seem to even know. It seemed like he was no more aware of his solitude than was the rock itself. Time after time he would appear at the top of the rock, grin whole-faced, then drop on his bottom and slide down. He would disappear in the pool at the bottom, then pop up like a seal, gurgling, spitting out the cold water. Then he'd go and do it all over again, seeming never to stop for a breath. Such complete contentment with solitude was not natural, Susan thought, then she wondered how she had become so cynical.

She asked the lifeguard about him. Yes, she'd seen the boy there before, and no, he was never with anyone. No, she'd never noticed anyone dropping him off or coming to claim him at the end of the day. He was not one of the park ranger's kids, the lifeguard said. If he was, she would know him. Maybe a parent drops him off at the entrance and comes back for him at the end of the day. She'd like to catch them doing that. How did they expect her to be a lifeguard and a babysitter at the same time? Not that she'd ever had trouble out of that one. No, he just plays and plays, always by himself.

At one o'clock Susan called Sam out of the water. He wanted to keep going and started to get whiney. She toweled him off and assured him he could do it again, but he needed to rest awhile first and have some lunch. The loner boy had just come up from the pool and stood at the bottom of the rock, rubbing his eyes with the back of his hands. Susan's heart wrenched. She took Sam by the shoulders, turned him around, and nodded toward the boy. "Go over and ask him to come have lunch with us."

He crinkled up his nose. "How come?"

"Because it looks like he's all by himself. Go on."

He scowled, and with eyes hooded, the towel hung over his head, he plodded toward the boy. He mumbled something to the boy and pointed, still frowning, toward Susan. She smiled and nodded, the other boy shrugged, and soon the three of them had found a small clearing in the woods nearby. She spread a blanket, and the boys ate peanut butter and jelly sandwiches in stubborn silence, until she took out egg salad and Sam wrinkled up his nose and, boy-like, said something impolite about the source of the smell. The boy sniggered.

That broke the ice. What was his name? Bo. Where did he live? Where did he go to school?

"Over by Muddy Creek," he said, in answer to both questions. That didn't tell her much.

She had brought along dirt cake, a messy confection she made from crumbled chocolate cake and pudding, with gummy worms "crawling" inside it. Bo claimed he'd never seen gummy worms before. Sam couldn't believe it.

"Bet you never seen one of these before!" Bo said, then opened his cavern of a mouth wide to show Sam the cake-covered gold tooth at the back. After that they climbed trees, swung like apes, tried to see who could spit the farthest. They surprised her with a rattlesnake skin Bo found near the creek. She acted appalled at the sight of it, knowing they expected it of her.

"Aw, old snakeskin never hurt nobody," Bo said, grinning.

She asked Bo if he lived with both his parents. No answer. His eyes darkened. He shrugged. Was he cared for by a grandparent, maybe? No answer.

She let them slide for another couple of hours. The day passed quickly. It was a while until dark, but it became dusky very quickly under the dense foliage, in the shadow of the mountains. Kids and parents left the rock and filed, trailing water, through the bathhouse out to the parking lot. Susan had not come prepared to spend the night away from home, and they had a three-hour drive ahead. She had to think about leaving.

"Come on, you two. Time to pack it up. And you, Bo, we better get you home." But he didn't want to go home, he said. She took him by the shoulders, looked him in the eyes. Children suffered in this world, more in their own homes and among their own kin than anywhere, and she looked for signs of it in his eyes. "Why, Bo? Why don't you want to go home?" He turned away. "Look, now. You're putting us in a tough position, you understand. We can't leave and let you stay out here by yourself all night."

He shook his head. Yes, you can, he said. He did that all the time.

"Well, that we are not going to do," she said.

It was better than going home, he said. Anything was. Could he go home with them? Oh, she wished he could, but she could hardly pluck someone's child out of the air and claim him, could she? She wondered later what it might have been like if she had.

"Come on, Bo. How about the people you live with, your parents, whoever? And think of Sam and me. Think of how we would feel driving off and leaving you here. We are going to get you home."

Their picnic things packed in the trunk and the boys settled in the backseat, she asked him, "Alright now, which way?

"That way," he said and pointed north.

She sighed. "You're sure of the way?" He was sure, he said. If she drove that direction and missed a turn she could wind for miles on the scenic byway, could end up on the Parkway and wind some more. They might be past midnight getting home. She unfolded a map, put on reading glasses, and studied the tiny squiggly lines representing mountain roads.

"I don't see any place called Muddy Creek," she said. He shrugged, and she realized, while dragging her finger across the map, that every nook and cranny, ridge, hill, cove, or creek in those hills might have a name, and they couldn't all be on a map. She eyed him in the rearview mirror. "Now, you'll tell me when to turn, won't you?"

He nodded, grinned. The two boys sat in the backseat, quiet now, tired right down to their bones. It would have made a good snapshot, Sam as pale and husky as Bo was brown and slight. After two or three miles she asked him if she was still going the right way.

"Yeah," was his only reply.

Susan sighed and draped her wrist across the steering wheel. The road wound and wound through darkening tunnels made by trees meeting overhead. Here and there leaves had turned brown and sourwoods had prematurely started to turn red because of the summer drought. The sun had slid behind a mountain somewhere. They'd driven a good fifteen minutes when Bo sat up in the seat and pointed to a side road she would have passed right by. "That way," he said. They drove on and on until Sam said, "I gotta go."

"Well, it looks like the side of the road will have to do," she said.

"But I want something to drink, too."

"Well, you'll just have to wait for that," she said.

"There's a store at the crossroads," Bo said. "Just up the road." Well, that was welcome news, some small confirmation that he knew where he was going.

She pulled into the Gas, Gobble, and Go. In the store Sam went straight for the MoonPies. Susan told him if he had to "go" so bad, he ought to do that first.

"Back there," said the teenage boy slouched behind the counter. He had pimples and a sunken chest. The toilet was inside the building, at the back of a short hall. It was well within her sight, so she let Sam go alone. She talked Bo into getting something for himself, a Pepsi from the ice chest, a pack of salted peanuts. He dumped the peanuts into the Pepsi first thing. Sam came back. Bo burped, grinned. She took the bottle from him. "You go on and go, too," she told him, and told Sam to keep an eye on him.

Outside, she filled the tank with gas and washed the windshield. She went back into the store. "Alright boys, let's hustle!" she said. But Bo was not there. She paid for the gas and everything the boys had picked out. "Where'd Bo go?"

"He's in the bathroom," Sam said.

"Still?"

Sam checked again. The teenage boy checked. No Bo. He bet he went out that way, the boy said, pointing toward the back door situated between the men's and women's rest rooms.

They looked everywhere. Around the back of the building, both ways up the road. They traipsed into the woods calling and calling. Back in the store and down every aisle again, behind every shelf. They looked in the big ice chests where all the sodas and ice cream treats were kept. Then they waited and looked again. She felt sick. "This is awful. . . . Awful. What if he's been kidnapped?"

The boy shook his head. "Don't see how he could've been kidnapped. Nobody been in or around here since y'all drove up. I figure he must've decided to go home on his own."

She would hope so, but she doubted it. He had so dreaded going home. And if he had gone home, what to?

"Where's Muddy Creek?"

"It's a mud hole right across the Jackson County line," the boy said. He told her to go to this crossroads and around that curve, and up this ridge and down that hill. She pressed her fingers to her temples, trying to take it all in. "Don't be looking for a sign that says 'Muddy Creek,'" he said. "There ain't one. A sign that is."

"Then how will I know when I'm there?"

"You'll dead-end into a muddy creek."

She repeated the directions back to him. "How far is it?"

"Two-and-a-half, maybe three miles, I'd say, as the crow flies. It'd be one heck of a walk. Only way he'd be there now is if he flew there in a plane."

"Maybe we'll see him on the road, then. If not, maybe somebody there will know where to look for him."

He shook his head. "Good luck. When I was with the rescue squad I answered a call back in there. There was just one house, and nobody lived there but a grouchy old woman and her invalid brother."

In a little while they came to a hog path of a road that descended to the banks of what might sometimes be a wide creek. Because of the drought it was low; puddles rested among the rocks in the creek bed. They passed an abandoned shack; beyond it, where the creek made a sharp turn, stood a bungalow made of shingle and stone. A roof hung low over a wraparound porch. Somebody sat in a chair on the front porch. From the distance it looked like someone of considerable age, with a blanket thrown over knees and feet. In a clearing around one side of the house, a woman stood with her back to them, taking clothes from a line. She looked up when she heard the car, but then went back to her folding and stacking. They walked her way, but she heaved the clothes basket on her hip and started toward the front porch. Susan took Sam by the hand and met the woman halfway across the yard. Elephantine legs showed under a flower-printed housedress. She repositioned the basket on her hips and glanced sideways at them. "So? What do you want?"

"I need your help. I'm looking for a lost boy."

She stopped. "It yours?"

"No, I—"

"Then what concern is it of yours?"

"What concerns me," Susan said, "and what I think would concern anybody with half a heart, is a lost child." The woman looked like she'd been slapped. "He must belong to somebody around here," Susan said. "He said he was from here."

A little glint came up in the woman's eyes. She looked at Susan a long time. "Well, I can't help what he says," she said and waddled toward the house. Just then a keening—a pathetic, stifled wail—came from the porch. The woman stopped, looked toward the porch, and dropped her shoulders in exasperation. Then she turned around and faced them, wearily. "He's done seen the boy, now," she said accusingly. "Come on then." Susan followed her across the yard and up the steps, pulling Sam behind her.

The disabled man was sitting in a chair at the far end of the long porch. His head was slumped sideways into his neck. It disturbed her how bright his eyes were in the pale, slack face. She thought he might be in his late fifties or early sixties. A plastic bowl of peanuts sat on his lap. Susan couldn't see that he was capable of eating them.

"My brother, Herman," the woman said.

Susan took his hand. It was like taking hold of a handkerchief, but there was strength in his eyes. She thought he was glad to have company. She introduced herself and Sam.

"And your name?" Susan asked the woman.

"Aida," she said, begrudgingly.

"Look!" Sam said. A white squirrel inched across the windowsill, jumped on Herman's bony shoulder, reached down, and took a peanut. It sprang back and sat cracking and nibbling the nut. "That squirrel's just about the only friend he's got," Aida said. "He likes to show him off." Susan thought she was softening somewhat, but she turned to Susan and looked her hard in the face. "People don't know what all I have to put up with," she said. "I can't hardly handle what all I've got."

Sam stayed with Herman and the pet squirrel while Susan accompanied the woman into the front parlor. It was small, with too much furniture. Plates hung close to the ceiling. There was nothing to suggest a child had ever lived there, no toy trucks, no muddy shoes. Through a window partly covered with a lace curtain she could see Herman's slumped frame. Sam stood at his shoulder, cautiously handing a peanut to the white squirrel.

The woman dumped the basket of clothes on a side chair. She motioned for Susan to sit. Susan continued to stand. "Look, Aida," Susan said. "Let me have my say and if you can't help us we'll leave." She explained how they'd met the mischievous little boy at Sliding Rock, the boy and her son became fast friends, nobody came for him, she insisted on taking him home. They stopped at a corner store, and the boy had disappeared. For some reason, he ran away. It was clear he didn't want to come home. She looked around. "This is where he told us he lived," she said. "And if it's not where he lives, and you can't tell me where he might be, I'll have to go to the police."

Her eyes flared at the mention of the police. "Don't matter if you do or if you don't. Sheriff won't pay you half a mind. He knows country boys ain't like your city boy, having to hang on to their mama's skirt tails. That boy knowed how to get home. You take my word for that. He got home." She seemed certain.

"That doesn't make me feel a whole lot better. Home wasn't much of a place, the way he talked."

Aida's eyes went dark. "That worries you, don't it?"

"Yes."

She looked at Susan a long time. She started to speak, but her voice broke. "I don't know how much more I can handle," she said. She wiped her eyes with the tail of her apron. "Alright. Wait a minute." She disappeared into a back room.

While she was gone, Susan pulled back the lace curtain and saw Sam now sitting at Herman's feet, cracking the peanuts to save the squirrel the trouble. It was early evening and the sun had gone behind a cloud. The parlor and the kitchen beyond were dim now.

Aida came back and motioned Susan toward the couch. She switched on a lamp, and the slumped figure outside the window darkened to a silhouette. The squirrel on his shoulder looked spectral. Aida sat next to Susan and opened an old photo album. "This was my brother before he got in the shape he's in now," she said.

Susan pulled the photo album closer and looked at the pictures. The pictures were black and white, overexposed, and faded with time. She couldn't tell much about Herman's face or features, but what he had once loved to do was evident. He had been energetic, athletic.

"Here's a picture of him climbing up Looking Glass Rock," Aida said. "And here he is at the top of Devil's Courthouse. That's where he fell, back in '68. He'd always been scrawny looking, but he was strong. They always said he was a good, careful climber, but all it takes is one slip of the foot. . . ." Her voice broke again. "He's been paralyzed from the waist down ever since."

"That's very sad," Susan said. "I'm sorry to hear it."

"He's never been the same since. Nothing has ever been the same. I've spent my life taking care of him, and I don't regret it, but it's getting to where I can't keep him here. I'm getting too old and feeble myself. I'm going to have to put him somewhere, and it'll kill my soul to do it."

Aida pointed to a snapshot at the bottom of the page and went on. "He never cared much for hunting, but he loved to fish for trout." The picture was of a young man in his twenties. Tall, dark, thin, holding up a fish on a line. "And here he is, before the accident, rafting on the French Broad River. He loved the water more than anything in this world."

"I can see that he did," Susan said. "It's an awfully sad thing."

"You said you were at Sliding Rock today, you and your

boy. We used to go there, all of us, the whole family. We used to know the people who owned the land, before the public even knew about it. Had to hike through the woods for a mile to get there. Here's a picture of all of us there. That's me standing next to Herman, when we were little." The family in the photograph looked like any family in faded snapshots from the early '50s, generic faces and bodies fish-belly white.

Whoever had taken the picture had stood as far back as possible to get everything in; the granite rocks, the falls, the mountain laurel, everything and everybody blended together in two shades of gray. The picture was of everyone and no one. A photograph of ghosts, made from a safe distance. Aida pointed out a much thinner version of herself, in a skirted swimsuit and bathing cap. Her head was inclined to the side, and she held the hand of a boy, younger and shorter than in the previous pictures.

"That one might look familiar to you," she said. Strangely, it did. Aida turned another page. "And here's another one of him, by himself."

At the bottom corner, in a picture barely stuck on the page by two pieces of yellowed transparent tape, was another faded image, a photograph that was many years older than the ones she'd shown yet, but it was close-up, and she could read the features. It was of a boy, not a young man. The woman watched Susan lift the edge of the page and lean closer. "I don't understand," Susan said.

"Neither do I," Aida said. There, with the tangle of mountain laurel and the long low slope of Sliding Rock as a backdrop, was the unmistakable image of the lost little boy.

"I was just over two years old when Bo was born," the woman said. "When Herman was little we called him Bo. I got it started, couldn't say 'brother' or even 'bro' so it came out 'Bo.' You know how that is.

"Anyhow, he was born too little. He almost died once. But Mama fed him sassafras and sourwood honey and prayed over him until he started to thrive. I looked after him. He was my pet then like he is now."

"I still don't understand."

"I'm not surprised at that," she said, closing the picture album. "None of them ever do."

"Who doesn't?"

"The ones who come here, like you, after they've seen him. People drive up just like you did a while ago. More often than not, though, they're people my age or older, ones from around here, who knew Bo back when. 'We saw a boy who was the spittin' image of Bo at fifteen,' they'll say. They say they've seen him rafting at the river or fishing for trout, or hiking a trail in the woods. I just shake my head and say maybe he's got a double. I've heard tell we've all got a double somewhere.

"But every once in a long while somebody'll come by here who has seen Bo as a little boy, playing at the swimmin' hole, or swinging on a tire swing in somebody's backyard, or at the creek trying to catch salamanders. Or, like you did, they'll see him slipping and sliding at the sliding rock. Just like you they try to take him home, just like you they push and push and make me tell them, but they never believe. It's happened over and over again and they never a one of them believe. It ain't a good feeling to be made out a liar, or for somebody to think you're just a dumb old hillbilly woman. So I hate to see them come. Like I hated to see you come."

"I'm sorry."

"Don't you worry about it. Soon as you leave, I'll be alright. It'll settle on me that it don't much matter whether anybody believes or not. I know what I know. There was One who promised to make the lame to walk and the blind to see, and that One don't break His promises. I know there are ways to walk and ways to see that we know not of, that somehow, every once in a while, he finds his way out, Bo does, that little boy inside the man."

After they left, Susan was able tell Sam that Bo had found his way safely home.

"How do you know?"

"That woman told me."

"She knows him?"

"Yes, I would say she knows him very well."

The long winding mountain roads put him to sleep before

he could ask too many questions. She was glad of it. It would give her time to think of a way to explain to him what a strange and wonderful thing the mind is. Just like the creeks and the rivers, it can find ways to go great distances. It can wind its way through every kind of terrain, making rivulets and cutting ravines wherever it has to, to find its own path to freedom.

One Winter's TALE

There are those who confess belief in the supernatural. I, Agatha Prymme, have never been one of that number. The little incident that I am about to relate was simply, plainly, an episode of acute delirium, except for one small detail which I shall disclose, and for which I am certain I will discover a perfectly rational explanation before I leave this Earth.

It was early January of 18—, and I had just recovered—or I thought I had recovered—from a bout of typhoid. I had, I believed, bid a fond farewell to the dreadful fever, chills, malaise, and the lurid fancies that so often accompany that dread sickness. I had been warned by my doctor that I should stay abed until spring. Nevertheless, stubborn and ambitious soul that I am, I made plans to travel by train, in the dead of winter, southward into Kentucky, where I would assume a multitude of duties at a small mission church in the coal-mining community of Pine Ridge.

I had recently undone the last of three messy romantic entanglements and had dismissed, once and for all, the pursuit of matrimony. I had adopted the notion that spinsterhood was anything but the disease society made it out to be, and I had dismissed the notion that having limited resources would prohibit a full and satisfying life. I had intellect, industry, and thrift. I could work for myself, manage for myself! Spinsterhood could be, and would be for me, a state of heady freedom, an opportunity to roll up my sleeves and do some measurable good in a woefully broken and mismanaged world.

And blast the doctor's orders! He had assured me I was cured and no longer contagious, but he insisted I needed days, if not weeks, of bed rest to regain my strength and my mental dexterity. Poppycock! Work was what I needed to assure my complete recovery. Work! My fingers itched to be involved in meaningful labor towards the betterment of mankind.

I knew the people of Pine Ridge might resent the boisterous presence of an outsider such as myself. I knew that the tiny schoolhouse had been burnt to the ground because the pupils didn't like the previous teacher, and that the only medical care in the hollow was provided by an aged granny woman who was openly antagonistic toward modern medicine. None of this did I, Agatha Prymme, find the least bit daunting.

As the train chugged along the valleys of Kentucky's Cumberlands, I was more infused with enthusiasm with each passing mile. Here, where ignorance and superstition still cast as much darkness over the region as do the precipitous mountain peaks, what opportunities I would have to serve, to enlighten! My duties would be richly varied. I would use my nursing skills to educate the populace about matters of health and hygiene. I would teach the illiterate to read. I would play the piano at services and organize wholesome activities for the children. I would shine the bright light of reason in that dismal little corner of the world, where a flickering light in the night woods was still thought to be a corpse candle, where every dark curve along a mountain road was thought to be "hainted"!

By the time I arrived I was fatigued and travel worn, as I had not fully recovered from the fever. The wind hit hard and cold as I stepped off the train at the little station. It was a long step, for I am a woman who is very small in stature. I pulled my hood over my head, tightened my coat around my waist, tucked my hands into my pockets, and looked around, hoping to meet a friendly face or shake a warm hand. Alas, no one was there but a little mole of a man behind the counter and, slumped in a chair, a farmer type whose sole occupation seemed to be watching the trains come and go through the cracks in his eyelids.

The man who would be my landlord, a Mr. Odell, was supposed to be there to meet me. Now where was he? It was only midafternoon, but it was already quite dark. I knew that the sun, which had been well above the horizon as the train had made the final curve into Pine Ridge, must still be shining somewhere. The cold was chapping my thin cheeks, numbing my nose.

Finally Mr. Odell arrived, with no apology for being late. He was a stringbean of a man, in overalls, with stain of coal grit in his pores and under his fingernails. He introduced himself with a tip of his hat, loaded my trunk onto his wagon, and away we went. We drove along a narrow lane that meandered alongside a rush-and-tumble creek. Soon the sun slipped from its hiding place behind a mountain, and bold rays winked through the winter trees. I looked forward, after my full recovery, to brisk walks through those winter hills in addition to my regular rounds of calisthenics!

The little house I was to occupy stood in deep shade under old hemlocks, a situation which might be a delight in summer, but would make for a cold, cold winter. The house had one and only one interesting feature—a large, multipaned window, so large that it looked as if the window had been chosen and a house had been grudgingly built to accommodate it. Such a large window would be of no advantage for keeping the heat in, but it would at least let into the drab interior what bits of light managed to penetrate through the dense tree cover.

The landlord brought in my belongings and showed me a larder well stocked with potatoes, onions, and smoked meat. A trunk at the foot of the feather bed was filled with fresh, though rough-textured, linens, which more than satisfied me, as I am a woman of simple tastes. Mr. Odell started a fire in the woodstove, and from the doorway he pointed out the direction of his house, the ruins of the burnt schoolhouse, and the church. I peered through my spectacles with great effort, but due to a frosty mist hovering above the ground I was able to see plainly only the steeple and the ghostly outline of the building itself. The church was at the foot of the foremost mountain, and I could reach it by the road, but it was quicker to hike the half mile across the gently rolling field I saw before me. I told him I would be most anxious to make the trek the moment I regained my strength.

I needed a few days to settle and gain my fortitude, but I was anxious to see that the church, which would serve as a school until the schoolhouse was rebuilt, was well equipped for my every task. Furthermore, I took upon myself the role of sentry regarding the church, since it had not escaped my mind that the perpetrators of the schoolhouse fire might vent their wicked energies on the church as well.

I thanked Mr. Odell for his kindness, and watched as his wagon diminished into the evening shade and disappeared around the bend in the road. I stepped inside, and before I closed the door one snowflake fell and lay, patterned like a tiny lace doily, on the raglan sleeve of my gray coat. Another fell, and another. I shivered and closed the door, then settled in for a long and fruitful night by the fire.

Inside, I stoked the fire, chose a potato from the larder, and shoved it into the woodstove to bake for my supper. I was quite tired by the time I had unpacked my trunk and eaten my supper. I knew I must take it easy. The doctor may have been right: I was not strong yet, though he would never hear those words from my lips! So I sat down in the only easy chair in the room, which was situated right by the big, drafty, and cur-tainless window and was, unfortunately, too heavy for me to move.

I draped a quilt across my lap and took up needle and thread to reinforce the pocket lining of my coat. I had found the coat in a consignment shop some years earlier. Though it was made of cashmere, it was a drab gray color, the inner lin-ing was already Swiss-cheesed by moths when I bought it, and in the years I had owned it the surface had worn natty. Still, I appreciated the coat for its practicality, for the full sleeves and large hood.

The task quickly and efficiently done, I tied the last knot in the thread, stuck the needle into the pin cushion, and put pen to paper to sketch out some preliminary lesson plans.

Some time passed. It had gotten colder. I drew the quilt up around me, looked out the big, east-facing window, and watched the night deepen behind a white curtain of snow. The house shuddered and cracked with the rising wind. I smiled, almost understanding, for the first time, how simple people in such rural isolation might misinterpret the whining wind as a screaming hag, a wailing banshee! But knowing it was only the wind, I drowsed.

Sometime later the icy draft in the room nudged me to wakefulness. I came up slowly out of sleep, dreaming I was climbing up out of a snowdrift, little knowing, at that moment, how nearly prophetic was that dream. I touched my fingertips to my forehead. It was hot with fever and damp with perspiration. I knew it! I knew I would catch my death sitting next to that enormous drafty window. I would demand that my landlord seal the cracks around it, and I would take it upon myself to sew up heavy draperies. The fire had died down to a single stingy burning ember. My lamp, which had burned down to a mere quivering speck, wavered in a sudden draft, and died. I drew my knees up to my chest and yanked the quilt up to my neck.

The room was dark, the window bright. The snow billowed like sheets hung on a line. I was entranced. The wind momentarily subsided, and tiny lights waved and flickered near the foot of the mountain. Another gust and the lights were hidden, another lull and they flickered and wagged like red-gold tongues again. Was it my landlord, wielding a lantern, bringing more firewood? Surely he would come by wagon, along the road instead of across the field. A few moments passed. No one came. The lights still burned, waved, flickered, now lesser, now greater. A service at the church? No, not on a weekday evening, and not in such awful weather. A fire! At that very moment, as I sat in idle speculation, flames could be licking their way down the aisle and up the altar! Heaven help us all! Could the vandals not wait a week?! I flew up out of my chair, hastily lit a lantern, and, by its light, put on boots and coat. I took hold of the lantern, raised the hood of my coat over my head, and opened the door to the swirling white.

The icy wind slapped at my face, once, twice. I stepped forward over the threshold, under the dark canopy of hemlocks, and into the wide-open, rolling field. The wind punished me for my boldness. It whipped at me from all sides and yanked back the hood of my coat. I drew it back up again and only then realized I had forgotten gloves. For some distance I wandered along snow-blind. I strayed into hillier terrain and sank to my knees in a drift. I struggled to my feet. With one cruel swipe the wind stripped the hillside of fallen snow, heaved it upon me, and snuffed out my lantern. White, white, nothing but white. How far had I come? Which way forward, backward?

I fell again, but this time against a stout tree trunk. I clamped my eyes shut against the snow. The downy flakes felt like stinging pellets on my bare hands and face. I opened my eyes and, though the snow still fell, the wind subsided for the moment. Just ahead lights flickered and waved from the pointed windows of a small church. Candles in the windows, no doubt! What an unexpected and charming sight! It was as if a curtain had been pulled back to show a little set in a theater. Singing voices wafted from inside, now full, now soft, buffeted about with every gust of wind. A choir at practice! With the little mystery dispelled, my fear and anguish subsided. Now to warmth, to shelter!

I struggled to my feet and rushed forward to the wooden door. The heavy door was tightly closed, and, like the windows, arched into a point. No light penetrated from beneath it or from around its edges. So frozen was my hand I was unable to bend my fingers to try the handle. I beat lamely with my knuckles for some time. The door creaked open. The singing voices resounded. The narrow crack between the door and its jamb blazed like a long wand of golden light.

A man's face appeared, a long face, lined deep as a peach pit. His nose was misshapen like a candle left too near a fire. His eyes were filmy and vacant, as the eyes of very old men so often are. "Come in, my dear lady!" he said. "Come in out of that awful weather!"

I stepped into a dragon's breath of heat. I was glad for the warmth, but even then, frozen as I was, I could tell it would soon be stifling. In no time at all, or so it seemed, my coat, which had been smothered in snow, turned into a dripping woolen mass. Water dripped from the hood into my face, and I was chilled all over again.

The old man helped me remove the coat. He shook it out and hung it carefully on a peg against the wall, where other coats, homelier, nattier than my own, had been hung. I wondered how the single potbellied stove in the tiny sanctuary, which I could see from the small opening at the back of the vestibule, could warm the place so profoundly. I rubbed my hands together, blew on them. "How dedicated you all are to come out in this weather!" I said, just loud enough to be heard over the singing.

"Oh, we don't let anything stop us from our yearly singin'!" he whispered back. "Not anything in this world!" So it was not a choir practice I had stumbled upon, but a hymn singing.

I peeped inside the open archway into the small sanctuary. In the far corner, behind the altar, stood the piano I would be privileged to play at some future time. The walls of the nave had been built of rough-hewn timbers. In the sills of the pointed windows sat stout beeswax candles, no doubt the source of the lights I'd seen from my house. Between rows of empty wooden pews and the altar, ten maybe twelve people sat on plank benches which had been arranged in a square. All were humbly dressed, the women in well-worn homespun and bonnets, the men in either tattered overalls or Sunday suits. All heads were bent in rapt study of the open books— which I took to be hymnbooks—in their laps. As they sang they all looked up now and again to the song leader who stood before them.

The song leader was a tall man with scarecrow hair, dressed like a preacher. He held up a wide-open hymnal in his left hand while his right arm swung upward, downward, outward, upward, downward, outward as he led the small group in a style of a cappella singing that I, with my varied musical background, recognized at once as "singing the shapes." I knew that the singers, like their leader, were following in the hymnbooks a simple hieroglyphic of small notes: squares, circles, and triangles. It was a method used to teach hymn singing to rural people, most of whom did not read standard musical notation.

The primitive a cappella singing made for a rich, haunting sound that delighted the ear and stirred the soul to the depths. I also knew from my experience that visitors were encouraged to participate. At another time I would be happily swept up into the fray, but at that moment, weak and feverish, not to mention hatless and disheveled, I wanted only to slip quietly into a pew near the back. When I had sufficiently warmed myself and regained my strength, I would slip back out again and make my way home. But my greeter took me by the arm. "You must join us," he said, insistence burning in his eyes.

"Oh, no! Please!" I whispered, pleaded, pressed my fingers together in supplication. "Just let me sit there awhile." I pointed to a pew near the back. "Just let me sit right there and listen!" He nodded in agreement and released my arm. He went and poked at the fire in the woodstove, which I presumed was his main purpose besides manning the door. I chose a moment when the song leader's eyes bore down on the hymnbook, then I slipped into a pew near the back. It was one of those rare times when my short stature is of benefit: I was able to slump down in the pew and remain hidden, or so I imagined.

All this time the a cappella voices in the small sanctuary had been rising and falling. "We sing of the land of the blest!" they sang. "That country so bright and so fair!" Such force and power from such few voices! How the little sanctuary reverberated with the swell of voices, as if the walls would give way and the roof itself would fly off! "All hail that bright morning, all hail that new day! When with loud shouts of glory we'll all fly away!" The hypnotic swinging of the song leader's arms, the lurid flickering candlelight! Small wonder I was afterwards convinced that the whole event, down to every last detail, had spun solely from my delirium!

The night wore on. I wanted to leave but lacked the strength. I felt ever more feverish. My corset and petticoats stuck to my skin like hungry leeches. As I sat slumped in my pew with my damp head in my sweating palms, the words of the songs became increasingly melancholy. The mood of the singers matched the dying of the fire in the woodstove, the sputtering of the candles in the windowsills. The song leader's shoulders slumped, he flipped wearily through the hymnbook, and his voice took on a funereal tone. They sang of "the land of ceaseless shade," and of "that dreary region of the dead where all things are forgot." Heaven help us!

"Now, brother," a bonneted woman from the group asked the song leader, in a voice so tired I thought surely it would be the last words she ever spoke, "how come we have to sing those ole mournful songs?"

"Mournful suits the situation," the song leader said.

"Can't argue with that," another man from the group said. There followed a begrudging mumble of agreement among the crowd. Then they began to sing, in voices slow and halting, as if pushing a coffin uphill, as if stopping to dig a grave between each word: "Shall this weary body turn to dust? And in its lonesome grave till Judgment lie?"

Oh! Such a dreary tune! I covered my ears to keep from hearing all the words to it. They came at last to the end of the final verse. As if to mark the moment, the flame of the last burning candle, long ago shrunk to a puddle in a window near the altar, died. It extinguished itself as swiftly and as surely as if some invisible someone, weary of the proceedings, had crept up to the candle, pressed thumb and forefinger together around the pinhead flame at the end of the wick and—pfft!—snuffed it out!

Now we all sat in near darkness. The only light came from the woodstove and the snow-lit windows. Just enough light shined that I could see their faces, now deflated, their bodies, now leached of all vitality.

"We all know our time is up," the song leader said. "They's no use looking all sad faced about it. Let's go on now and sing our parting hymn. We all know that one by heart." He lifted and swung his arm, and the singing began. I chose that moment to slip out of my pew into the aisle. The leader's arm froze in midair. The voices fell. He watched me. They all turned to look at me. I shall never forget those faces, some bovine and welcoming, others stern, suspicious. There were two young pale faces, the eyes blinking rapidly, but most were faces creased with age and drawn with fatigue. Faces tired and yet, at the same time, so eager. Yes. All so eager! "Come on and join in with us, sister," the minister said. "Help us sing our parting hymn."

"Oh, no!" I said, mumbling the first excuse that came to my mind, and a falsehood at that. "I . . . I'm afraid I'm quite tone-deaf!"

"I think our guest ought to join us in our parting hymn," he told the group again. "What do you all say to that?" There was a mumble of approval. They all stood, turned, and bumbled against each other, rushing in my direction, bouncing off each other with a peculiar light buoyancy. Such frail bodies, their skeletons light as bird bones bound together with ligaments and sinews of cobwebs!

"No!" I screamed. "No!" And at that precise moment the front door opened and a whoosh of bitterly cold air filled the sanctuary. The bodies were yanked upward like puppets on strings and swirled like figures in a mobile high in the peak of the nave. I covered my face with my hands, fell over in a swoon, and knew nothing until, sometime later, I awoke to find myself lying on my side in the church pew, in total darkness.

I sat up. I was alone in the cold church, alone with only the scent of raw air and the ever-so-faint scent of snuffed candles. It was dark except for the reflected glow of the white world outside. The windows framed the snowy landscape. I sat numbed by the cold yet mesmerized by the unearthly and lovely sight. Snow continued to fall outside the windows. Then the walls began to fade away. The snow was all around me, falling from above, from the high peak of the nave. I looked up, and though the snow still fell, a small space appeared between thinning clouds, and a few sparkling stars shone through. I was sitting not on a church pew, but on a bench made by a fallen tree in the winter woods.

I struggled back across the field, damp, feverish, numb with cold. How grateful I was to see my little hemlock grove, the branches bent with snow. The little house looked like gingerbread, its roof laden with scalloped icing along the eaves! Inside I threw a log into the woodstove, stoked the fire, removed my wet clothes, and put on my thickest wool dressing gown. I covered myself with a mass of quilts against the cold. The way I felt, I was certain that the bed would be the last place I would lie before I lay in my coffin.

But I awoke! I awoke in a pool of perspiration, to the fragrance of brewing coffee and burning wood. Mr. Odell towered over me, tall as a loblolly pine. The scent of cut wood and outdoor air was all around him. Beside him stood a rather prune-faced woman with shifty eyes, who I would learn was his wife.

On a stool by the bed sat an aged granny woman, hair gray as the wintry sky and stiff as a hearth broom. She fairly beamed when she told me that the acorn she had placed under my back had broken my fever. She informed me that having me breathe into the mouth of a toad was her preferred cure for fever, but it was, unfortunately, impossible to procure a toad that time of the year. At that revelation I fell back on my pillow and stared at the ceiling. Such superstitious nonsense! I had much work to do!

My landlord then told me how he, his wife, and the granny woman had come to be there. He had come the night of the snowstorm to bring me firewood, and, having been unable to get me to the door, had let himself in. Then, unable to wake me, he had gone to retrieve his wife and the granny woman, and had rushed with them to my bedside. I had been unconscious for the better part of two days! The granny woman chastised me for being out in the weather, but I declared that I had not been outside. I said this with all honesty, because I firmly believed that on that night, feeling cold and feverish, I had gotten up from my chair and gone straight to bed. Everything in between was no more than a hideous nightmare, or a lurid episode of typhoid delirium. And I told them all as much.

"Beggin' your pardon, Miss Prymme," Mr. Odell said. "You must've gone out for a little bit sometime after it took to snowin'. Y'see, when I came to the door with the load of fire-wood, there was footprints going out the house way out into the field yonder. And just inside the door was a puddle around where you left off your boots."

"I never once left this house!" I declared. I resisted the sip of moonshine and sourwood honey the granny woman put to my lips, and, feeling faint again, fell back onto my pillow and into another deep and thankfully dreamless sleep.

There followed several days of brutal cold. I sat in my chair by the fire. When I regained my appetite, I partook of some chicken soup Mrs. Odell, she of the prune face and shifty eyes, was gracious enough to bring to me. Soon the fog had cleared from my mind, I had the house to myself again, and was up on my feet. I felt weak but otherwise on the mend. It was Sunday morning. The sun shone with hard crystalline brilliance over the landscape. It was warming up. The icicles on the eaves were dripping. There was not the slightest breeze. I poked my head out the door and was amazed by the warmth. The church bells rang, and I thought the short walk to the church in such fair weather would do me more good than harm. I welcomed the opportunity to mix with company and go to the actual church, which I had not yet seen.

I had decided! I would go to the service. But I must hurry! Quickly, I pinned up my hair, laid out my boots, gloves, and scarf. But I missed my coat. I looked the small house over and could not find it. All the while I entertained the ungracious thought that maybe Mrs. Odell had taken it, thinking I might not fully recover my faculties enough to miss it. It was the kind of garment that a poor country woman might consider luxurious. Well, I could not openly accuse her, and I could not be bothered with the notion now, or I would be late. I hurriedly pinned on my hat, put on boots and gloves, and slipped on a loose-fitting cloth cape that would serve me well enough for the short walk to the church on this windless Sunday morning.

When I reached the church it was a delight to my eyes. Snow-covered, it perched at the rise of the hill with the mountain behind it. It was not, of course, the church of my illusory adventure. It was larger, made of brick, and it had sensible, rectangular doors and windows. All the more confirmation— as if I needed it!—that I had never once been at this spot before. I walked up the steps to the front door. Of course the church in my little nightmare had no steps at all. The service was rather dull, but I was quite content with dull, thank you very much. There was a piano, but no pianist. It was good to know my services would be needed and, if I felt more robust next Sunday, I would be able and happy to play. There were numerous introductions, although some of my future pupils greeted me warily, as I had suspected some might. Invitations followed the service, including an invitation to Sunday dinner from the minister and his wife, which I politely declined, owing to my still delicate health, but I happily accepted for the following week.

Mr. Odell stayed behind to close up the church. I was fatigued and knew I should be on my way, but I couldn't resist playing a few notes on the piano, so I was the last person, other than my landlord, to leave the church. We passed small talk, he inquired about my health. I remarked about the lovely brick church building, and was interested to learn that he had a hand in its actual construction. "Took the better part of a year to raise this one up," he said, "after the other one burnt down."

"The other one?"

"There," he said, pointing to a cluster of thick laurel at the bottom of the hill. Several yards from where we stood, in the direction of my house, I could just make out what looked like piles of rubble overgrown by the laurel. "There's what's left of it. Built in 1799, that one was. Burned down in 1841." He closed and locked the church, and asked if I could make it home alright. I thanked him, and assured him I would make it the short distance to the house with no difficulty. He tipped his hat and promised to seal around my drafty window the following week and bring another load of firewood. He mounted his horse and rode away.

I walked down to the tangle of laurel and found the ruins of the old church building, which was now nothing more than a crumbling stone foundation brocaded with snow. I brushed aside the snow from a section of the wall and, feeling fatigued, sat down before starting my walk home. And there, on a low branch of an ash tree that had sprung up and grown flush against the stone foundation, dripping now with melting snow, hung my gray cashmere coat.

FOR FURTHER READING

Southeastern coastal and Appalachian folk culture

Feltwell, John and Neil Odenwald. *Live Oak Splendor: Gardens Along the Mississippi, From Natchez to New Orleans.* Dallas: Taylor Publishing, 1992.

Hurmence, Belinda, ed. *Before Freedom,When I Just Can Remember: Twenty-Seven Oral Histories From South Carolina Slaves.* Winston-Salem: John F. Blair, 1989.

Joslin, Michael and Ruth Joslin. *Mountain People, Places, and Ways: A Southern Appalachian Sampler.* Johnson City, Tenn.: The Overmountain Press, 1991.

McCoy, Edain. *In a Graveyard at Midnight: Folk Magic and Wisdom From the Heart of Appalachia.* St. Paul: Llewellyn Publications, 1995.

Pinckney, Roger. *Blue Roots: African-American Folk Magic of the Gullah People.* St. Paul: Llewellyn Publications, 2000.

Pringle, Elizabeth Allston. *A Woman Rice Planter.* Columbia: University of South Carolina Press, 1992.

Rhyne, Nancy. *Plantation Tales.* Orangeburg, S. C.: Sandlapper, 1989.

Sakowski, Carolyn. *Touring the Western North Carolina Backroads.* Winston-Salem: John F. Blair, 1996.

Vlach, John Michael. *Back of the Big House: The Architecture of Plantation Slavery.* Chapel Hill: University of North Carolina Press, 1993.

Background material about coastal geography and wildlife

Ballantine, Todd. *Tideland Treasure: The Naturalist's Guide to the Beaches and Salt Marshes of Hilton Head Island and the Southeastern Coast.* Columbia: University of South Carolina Press, 1991.

American and worldwide folk culture and religious belief

Bennett, Gillian. *"Alas, Poor Ghost!": Traditions of Belief in Story and Discourse.* Logan: Utah State University Press, 1999.

Brunvand, Jan Harold. *The Vanishing Hitchhiker: American Urban Legends and Their Meanings.* New York: W.W. Norton and Company, 1981.

Felton, D. *Haunted Greece and Rome: Ghost Stories from Classical Antiquity.* Austin: University of Texas Press, 1999.

Goldman, Emily and Carol Neiman. *Afterlife: The Complete Guide to Life After Death.* New York: Penguin Studio, 1994.

Meyer, Richard E., ed. *Cemeteries and Gravemarkers: Voices of American Culture.* Logan: Utah State University Press, 1992.

ML   10/
                                            02